The Successful
Teacher's Handbook

The Successful Teacher's Handbook

Creative Strategies for Engaging Your Students, Managing Your Classroom, and Thriving as an Educator

PAT HENSLEY, MSEd

National Board Certified, Exceptional Needs Specialist

LITTLE,
BROWN
LAB

Little, Brown and Company
Hachette Book Group
1290 Avenue of the Americas, New York, NY 10104
littlebrown.com

First Edition: June 2019

Little, Brown and Company is a division of Hachette Book Group, Inc. The Little, Brown name and logo are trademarks of Hachette Book Group, Inc.

The publisher is not responsible for websites (or their content) that are not owned by the publisher.

The Hachette Speakers Bureau provides a wide range of authors for speaking events. To find out more, go to hachettespeakersbureau.com or call (866) 376-6591.

Cover by Alyson Forbes

Interior design by Tandem Books

ISBN 978-0-316-42482-0
Library of Congress Cataloging-in-Publication has been applied for.

Contents

Contents

Introduction

I always wanted to be a teacher, ever since I was a small child. I remember I loved to play "school" and begged my parents to buy me school workbooks in the summer, so I could use them in my "class." I loved learning and I wanted everyone else to love it as I much as I did. I can't remember ever wanting to do anything but teach!

I applied to a university out of state and paid for school myself. I kept my eye on my goal and didn't let anything sidetrack me from it—and was so excited when I got my very first teaching position.

My very first day of teaching was terrifying but exciting at the same time. I remember one of my first students showing up on crutches. He'd had his leg amputated over the summer due to bone cancer, but he was wearing a prosthesis. I greeted him by telling him I was his new teacher. The next thing I knew, he'd whipped off his prosthesis and was chasing me around the room. It took me a few minutes before I realized that I was the *teacher* and I was in charge! I whipped around and faced him, put my hand out, and told him to stop! I put on my "teacher" hat and demanded that he have a seat in the desk I assigned for him. Amazingly, he did what I told him!

I realized then that my learning had not ended but was going to be a lifelong process. *I don't believe passionate teachers ever feel like they have learned everything possible to be most effective in the classroom.* They are constantly looking for ways to better engage students and help them achieve their goals. While my university did a great job preparing me for my career in teaching, book learning is very different from actual experience. It is like learning to drive a car from a book and then actually being behind the wheel. Student teaching was a great experience, but you always have the actual teacher guiding you along. When you become the teacher, you are the one who is supposed to be the "expert."

My first day on the job, I walked into my empty classroom thinking, "Where do I go from here? What do I do?" I didn't have a handbook or an instruction manual to help guide me, but I wish I had! Other than from student teaching, everything I learned was through my own trial and error. I always hoped that someday I would be able to help others learn from my mistakes.

This is why I wanted to write *The Successful Teacher's Handbook*. I wanted to share my experiences, good and bad, to help new or struggling teachers—or anyone looking to refresh their knowledge of teaching. I wanted others to learn from my mistakes without having to experience them on their own. Hopefully, this book will help other teachers enjoy teaching more and make them less likely to burn out.

There is no magic recipe for teaching. A lot depends on what works for you and how it works with your students. It will take time and experience for you to figure this balance out.

In this book, I want to talk about several topics that I believe are important to new teachers. In my opinion, classroom management is the biggest key to successful teaching. I will share different strategies that have been successful in my classrooms over the years and include sample activities that range from elementary school to high school levels. If an example of an activity seems too young or too old for your students, just give it a tweak to make it age appropriate.

Another important topic I discuss is using technology in the classroom. In today's society, you need to meet students on the playing field they are comfortable with. For today's kids, that means through technology. For kids who weren't raised with computers, their ability to use one will impact their place in the working world. Today our classrooms are so diverse that we need to make sure we are sensitive to everyone's unique qualities and circumstances. That's why every teacher needs to have culturally responsive teaching methods in their tool kit. In addition to culturally diverse students, you may have students with disabilities in your classroom and will need to know some strategies that will make working with them easier. At the beginning of your career, you may find that you are working with a co-teacher. Many new teachers struggle to work in a co-teaching relationship, and I hope my suggestions can make this collaboration easier and more successful. Another part of teaching that I think is vital is parent involvement in the classroom. As teachers, our main goal is the students' success in the classroom and in life—and we need to make sure that we are working as a team with students' parents or caregivers.

I have been a special-education teacher for more than thirty years. Over those years, I've developed methods and strategies that will work in any classroom. These flexible, adaptable principles will help you be the best teacher you can be, regardless of your prior experience or the grade level of your students.

Best of luck, and happy teaching,
Pat

CHAPTER ONE
Where Do I Begin?

On my first workday as a teacher, I attended all the required meetings where they go over the teacher handbook, school routines, and other administrative details. Then I showed up in my empty classroom and wondered—where do I start?

I was totally overwhelmed and didn't know what to do next. I learned quickly that that is a common feeling at the beginning of every year and most teachers feel that way! After some time, I got into a routine, and when this clicked, I made a list of what I should do so that it can help me at the beginning of every year. I was able to revise this each year as needed, but it usually shook me out of my paralysis and got me moving.

Getting Started in Your Classroom

In this chapter, I'm going to share all my routines for getting a school year started on the right foot, including the first things you need to do to prepare for both your first day of work as a teacher and for your first day in the classroom with your students. These include obtaining your roster, setting up your classroom, decorating your classroom, developing a behavior plan, planning class routines, conducting emergency drills, and having a great first day with students.

Roster

First things first—you will get a student roster. It helps to know how many students you will have so you can set up your classroom properly. The roster will also let you know if there are any students who have special educational requirements. Some students may be categorized as students with special needs and have an individual education plan including accommodations or modifications for the classroom. Once you have your roster, you can ask yourself if certain students need to sit in special positions. This will help you determine the arrangement of the students' desks. Once you arrange the desks, make a seating chart of where you want the students to sit. This will take care of any specific seating needs and will help you learn your students' names faster.

Student Files

Create a file for each of your students where you can keep signed forms, assignments, and any other paperwork you might need to refer to later. You can use a system of hanging folders or a binder to keep everything organized.

Classroom Furniture

Next you need to get furniture for your classroom. You need a teacher's desk, student desks, and a large table for group work. A bookcase is always nice too. Most classrooms will have these in the room when you arrive, but this is not always the case. You should put your teacher's desk in the front corner away from the classroom door. This keeps it out of the flow of traffic and makes sure you are not blocking the board in the front of the room. I typically start the year out with the students' desks in rows and assign the students to desks, usually alphabetically so I learn their names, with the exception of any students with specific needs. Doing this will allow you to see how the students behave and figure out which students work well together—and who you do not want seated near each other. Later, you can rearrange the seats and form the students into groups.

Classroom Decor

You want students to feel welcome and happy to be in your classroom, so your classroom decor can send an important message. First impressions are important. Everyone likes to come into a room that feels inviting and welcoming. Having a nicely decorated room that is also neat and organized helps students maintain a positive attitude, while a dull, undecorated classroom can make students feel that you don't really care about your environment, or that the class will be boring. On the other hand, chaos, clutter, or an over-decorated classroom can make students feel nervous and uncertain.

There are a number of things you can do to make your classroom feel both inviting and well-ordered. To start, I like to decorate the door with my name and a welcoming decoration. It helps students know they are entering the correct classroom when they first arrive. I always put my name at the top of the door. Then I cut out book shapes from construction paper and write each student's name on it to decorate the door. That way students see their name when they arrive.

In your classroom, there should be a clearly designated area for group work and another area for individual work. You might use a carpet to designate the group area. In younger grades, some teachers put small chairs in a circle. In older grades, there may be a large table with chairs around it.

When choosing decorations for the room, try to stick with color themes so there is harmony in the colors. If your colors are all over the place, that could feel chaotic and even be hard to look at. Colors on the cool side of the spectrum, such as blues, greens, and purples, can bring feelings of calm, while reds, oranges, and yellows can bring feelings of excitement and stimulation. You don't want calm colors in an area where you want lots of movement and activity, and you don't want stimulating colors in the area where you want quiet reading or soft music.

If you have bookshelves, keep books neatly organized on the shelves. Separate fiction and nonfiction books into different sections. If you have room for a reading corner, you might want to put a piece of carpet down or beanbag chairs for recreational reading time.

There should be an area for art supplies for project work. Have supplies neatly organized so that students can find them and then learn to put them back in the right places. Clear plastic tubs that are labeled help with organizing these things.

If you have bulletin boards set up on your walls, it is important to keep them decorated. If there are two bulletin boards in the room, it is great to have one as a motivational board and the other to display student work. Don't allow the bulletin boards to be too cluttered. Again, make sure you use the appropriate colors for the message you want to display.

Often, teachers plan a monthly theme for their bulletin boards ahead of time. Then you could keep your eye out for decorations or ideas for each month throughout the year. Some suggested themes are:

September: back to school
October: favorite subjects or autumn
November: Thanksgiving
December: winter and snow
January: New Year
February: Valentine's Day
March: St. Patrick's Day
April: kites and spring
May: flowers
June: summertime

Other topics that are good throughout the year include: the ocean, the forest, birds, the desert, underwater animals, mammals, reptiles, weather, and healthy eating. You can search Pinterest for more bulletin board ideas.

Many school supply stores sell borders that can frame the bulletin board and make it look neat and seasonally appropriate. Then you just arrange and staple your decorations in the middle of the board. You can buy premade items for your bulletin boards or you can make your own using construction paper. You can even have your students help you make the items for the board. Some students are artistic and like the idea of making something for the board. Others may enjoy finding things from magazines to staple to the board.

Students also enjoy helping you take down the old bulletin board if they have earned free time. By allowing students to help you, you are helping their self-concept. (A self-concept is what a person believes about himself, feels about his own value, and how he perceives himself. Helping a student develop a healthy self-concept will help them during times when they face obstacles. This will give them the strength to face challenges and believe that they can succeed in whatever they strive to do.) They will feel that you trust them to help. Many younger students work hard to earn the reward of being a "helper."

Behavior Plan

The next most important thing to do is to develop a behavior plan. A behavior plan is basically your classroom rules of appropriate behavior, along with rewards and consequences. Your rewards and consequences will help your students learn the appropriate behaviors that you expect in your classroom. This prevents chaos and confusion as your year progresses. If all your rules are followed, your class will go smoothly with few bumps in the road.

It doesn't matter what grade level or subject you teach; your behavior plan is vital to the success of your classroom. Once expectations and consequences are understood, students know their boundaries and teaching becomes easier. For more information on how to set up your behavior plan, see chapter three.

Planning Your Subjects

After you set up your behavior plan, you need to know what subjects you are teaching and what materials or textbooks you will need. You also need to see if there are curriculum expectations or timeline requirements. This will help you with planning lessons and give you the big picture of what students should achieve for the whole year. If you are in special education, this will involve reviewing an individual education plan (IEP). In general education, you will also need to know which of your students have an IEP and what accommodations or modifications are required for this student. Remember, this is not optional and is required by federal law. For detailed tips on lesson planning, see chapter five.

SPECIAL TIPS FOR STARTING AT A NEW SCHOOL

- Get a map of the school and learn where the public places are in relation to your classroom.
- Get a mentor teacher.
- Get to know the other new teachers.
- Learn who to go to for office supplies such as paper clips, staples, tape, etc.
- Learn where the copy machine is, the procedure for using it, and how to add paper. (It always runs out of paper when you are alone in the room and there is no one to show you how to add paper!)
- Keep a list of important phone numbers (the school, the district office, human resources office, who to call when you need a substitute).
- Learn emergency procedures.
- Make sure you have enough student desks, group tables, and a teacher desk.
- When you know who your students are, locate their addresses on a map so you will know how close they live to the school.

Mentorship

If you're in a new school, you can really hit the ground running with help from a mentor teacher. (If you don't have a mentor teacher, the best person to go to will be your department head.) When working with a mentor teacher, know that you may need to begin the relationship by asking them questions, as sometimes the mentor doesn't want to seem overbearing or intrusive and may wait until you ask for help. They may have specific information to give you or may assume you already know some things. If you have a question or don't understand something, don't be afraid to ask. Questions about school policies and school procedures are great to ask your mentor. As the school year progresses, you may have a specific problem that you need to address, and asking your mentor for advice is helpful. Remember, you don't need to follow the advice if you don't agree or don't feel comfortable with it, but it is always good to get another perspective if you are struggling with an issue.

Class Routines

Your class routine is made up of the things you repeat every day in class even though the actual assignments change. Setting up these routines in the beginning of the year will help students understand what is expected of them each class period. You should post this routine on a wall before your students arrive on their first day, so they know about it from the beginning and can reference it whenever needed. Here is an example of a class routine that I find works really well:

1. When students arrive, have a short opening assignment (a warm-up assignment lasting about five minutes) for them to do, which gives you time to take attendance or do any general "housekeeping" chores.
2. Collect any homework assignments or papers that you need.
3. Begin the day's lesson.
4. Give assignments—these may be either group or individual assignments.
5. Then give the closing or summary of the lesson.
6. Last, always try to leave the five minutes at the end of class for cleanup and new homework assignments or any other last-minute things that pop up.

Although the lessons and assignments may change, the routine stays the same. This helps all students, especially those with special needs, know what to expect every day.

EMERGENCY DRILLS

On the very first day of school, I met my new student who was diagnosed with autism. Unfortunately, our school had undergone renovations that summer and the dust set off the fire alarm at the beginning of class. I had met my class only five minutes before the alarm went off, so when it sounded, there was a lot of chaos. I gathered everyone together to evacuate the building. My student with autism had trouble with the chaos and the loud alarm, so he bolted out of the evacuation area, out of the school gates, and ran down the street. After leaving my class with other teachers, I ran after him, trying to get him to stop. This was a feat because I was dressed in a nice business suit and high heels. Luckily I was able to call the front office from my cell phone and request help. A minute later, a young assistant principal came running up beside me and told me he would take care of it. Boy, was I relieved! That was when I realized that I needed to have an emergency-drill plan in place before I even met my students. I couldn't wait until I met the students and reviewed procedures. I'm so glad that other teachers around me helped me out, but I never started the year unprepared again.

Before students arrive on the first day, you should always make sure you know how emergency drills are run and where your students need to go. You always think you will have time to review this with students and then one day you find out that you don't. When there is chaos, students will look to you for guidance. You should have an emergency bag stationed near the door. The emergency bag should include your current roster, a map of the school showing the route of evacuation for your class, a pen or pencil, and any forms that are required to notify the administration if you are missing any students. This way, when you have to evacuate the building, all you have to do is grab this bag.

Prioritize!

During your start-of-year preparations, things will inevitably pop up that you will need to do before the students arrive. You may suddenly realize that you don't have forms that need to be handed out on the first day, or you may not know the schedule for the first day, which is different from a normal schedule. To stay on top of all the details, keep a spiral notepad close by and make a list as these things come to mind, or as administrators ask for things. Beside them, write the due date or time. At the end of the day, you can prioritize this list and it won't be so overwhelming. Then, when you tackle the list, do one thing at a time in order. If you need to, you can add new things to the bottom of the list and review it again at the end of the day. Keep all of these lists in one notebook in case you need to refer to earlier lists later.

Once the year starts, being organized and prepared is key to being successful in the classroom. At the beginning of each day, do the same prioritization routine that you did at the beginning of the year: Make a list of what you need to do for that day. Then prioritize the list items. This helps you see the big picture for the day and ensures that you have all the materials you need available and organized. Even though maintaining this list is another thing you need to do, you can get more things done this way—and cut down on your stress!

Before leaving at the end of the day, get organized for the next day so there is no need to get to school early. I recommend staying at least three days ahead with gathering the materials you need. You never know when the copier may break down or an emergency will pop up. You might have trouble finding the materials you need, and starting early gives you time to hunt for them. If you already have the materials you need for that day, you know you are prepared.

Must-Have Materials
- writing/drawing utensils
- drawing paper/construction paper
- worksheets
- assessment tools
- stapler
- glue/paste
- scissors
- manipulatives (physical tools of teaching, such as coins, blocks, puzzles, etc.)
- technology devices
- accommodations for special-needs students

Know Your Colleagues

Get to know your colleagues. Make sure you know the people in your department because they can be very helpful. Be alert and recognize those who have positive personalities and try to get to know them better. Their positivity will rub off and help you during your tough times. In the same vein, look for those you feel veer toward the negative and avoid them while you are still trying to get used to your new teaching career or a new school. Sometimes people are negative for different reasons and can't help themselves, but negativity can also be contagious, and you don't want to feel this way as you get started. Stick together with others who are still excited about teaching and enthusiastic about learning new strategies. Sometimes you can get great ideas from these people and then just adjust their methods to fit your students' needs. I was able to get great ideas from people not just in my own department but from other departments as well. Sometimes I would even ask them how I could fit their great lesson into my own class and many were able to think of ways that I hadn't thought of.

Your First Day with Your Students

On my very first day of teaching, when the students were expected to arrive, my stomach was filled with butterflies. I wanted to do a good job and make a difference. I wanted the students to like me. I wanted my colleagues to like me. I wanted to be able to handle everything that might happen. I wanted the administration to not fire me for any stupid mistakes I might make. This was the moment I seemed to have waited my whole life for and here it was. What a great feeling! I was filled with dread and excitement at the same time.

On the first day of every year, I still felt the same way. Even with all my years of experience, I still got butterflies on the first day the students arrive. Part of it was natural and all about the fear of the unknown. I had no idea what the students would be like or how the year was going to go, but that was part of the thrill of being a teacher. Every year is going to be different and every student is going to be different. I believe when this feeling goes away, it is time to retire or find another job.

Remember, butterflies are a good thing!

Butterflies

When you get butterflies, take a few deep breaths. Try to think about the absolute worst thing that could happen. Usually, when you start to think about this, it helps to calm you down, because you realize it's really not that bad. Remember that you can do this job, and you were trained to do this job. No matter what happens, if you make a mistake, apologize and move on. Don't beat yourself up over the minor mistakes. Usually, your students are as nervous about meeting you as you are to meet them!

Don't forget to enjoy your first day. This is an exciting day for you and your students—make it count.

At the end of the day, reflect on how your day went. Make a list of the changes you need to make for tomorrow. Make a list of the questions you have to find the answers to.

AVOIDING BURNOUT

It may seem strange to talk about burnout right after discussing your first day, but too often new teachers burn out quickly. They start out all gung ho and overdo it, so before long they are tired, sick, worn-out, and discouraged. When you travel by airplane, flight attendants go through the emergency drill and encourage parents to make sure they put the oxygen mask on themselves before helping their child. It won't help the child at all if the parent becomes unconscious. This applies to the classroom teacher also. If the classroom teacher doesn't take care of his/her mental and physical health, the students are the ones who suffer.

After the first week, if you are working through lunch and taking lots of schoolwork home in the evening to grade, then you are not organizing your time properly. On rare occasions, you might have to do schoolwork at home, but this should not be a regular habit. You need to look at what you are doing that is causing you to bring work home and change this behavior. It is not good for your overall physical or mental health.

It is important that you eat healthy food on a regular basis. Living on fast food or junk food is not the way to keep yourself fueled up to teach effectively. You are also not setting a good example for your students if they see you eating this way. Lunchtime is important because it gives your body and mind a break. It lets you regroup for the rest of the day.

Drinking water is important for energy levels also. Many new teachers get urinary tract infections because they don't drink enough water—out of fear they may have to use the restroom in the middle of class. This is a natural fear and experienced teachers know how new teachers feel. Before school begins, ask your neighboring teacher if they would mind watching your class if you have to leave to use the restroom. Usually, you won't need their help, but knowing you have it takes some of the pressure off the possibility that it might happen. In fact, your colleague may be glad you asked because they may have the same need. Eventually, your body will get used to your schedule and it won't be a problem.

Exercise is also a great reliever of stress. You may feel that you don't have time to exercise, but this is important in keeping your energy levels up and your stress levels down. You don't have to join a gym or get a personal trainer. Take time to add thirty minutes to your daily routine to go for a walk. Turn your mind away from your job and appreciate your surroundings. Take a deep breath and enjoy the moment.

Work Smart

Don't fall into the trap of thinking the harder you work, the better teacher you will be. It is easy to get to work early, work through lunches, stay late after school, and then work all evening. This does not make you better; it just wears you out! The more tired you are, the easier it is to catch every germ flying around the school, and you will get sick. Eventually you will build up some immunity to the germs, but why make it easy on them? Eating healthy is also important for your immune system. If you skip lunches, you will not have the energy to do all that you need to do. Sometimes even a short lunch break will help you be more productive instead of spinning your wheels.

It is important to work smarter and not harder. Once you develop a good routine for yourself and get organized, the easier teaching will be. Without a routine and organization that works for you, you will find yourself falling behind and quickly become overwhelmed. This is not the image you want your administrators to see! I see many new great teachers fall into this trap, and within a few years, they get burned out and leave the teaching profession. They were great teachers in the classroom and I hate that we lose them to other professions.

The Art of Standing Up at the Front of the Classroom

Picture this: It is now the first day of school. The students have arrived and are at their desks. They are all looking at you expectantly, waiting for you to speak your first words. Some of the students look eager to learn and others look like wolves ready to pounce on you if you show weakness. You can hear the silence in the room except for your heart beating loudly in your own ears. You wonder if the students can hear it. The butterflies in your stomach are fluttering like crazy and you feel as if you are going to either pass out or throw up.

Then you take a deep breath and settle down. You are the "expert" in the room and you are going to change lives. Maybe not today, but in the future. You will make a difference in these students' lives and you want it to be a positive difference.

It is tough to get up in the front of a room and start to teach. Every time you do it, you need to put on your "teacher hat." You have to mentally prepare yourself to be "on," and you will need to do this every day you teach. This may sound daunting, but it's part of the thrill of being a teacher.

Before the students arrive, always get in front of a mirror and check your clothes and your face to make sure everything is in order. You don't want students to see food in your teeth or your hair sticking up. Nothing can be more embarrassing than to find out later you didn't have a button buttoned or a zipper zipped.

If you are afraid you will forget something or the order that you want to follow, have an agenda written on the board for everyone, including you, to follow. This helps you stay on task and not get off track when talking to the students. Students love to get teachers sidetracked from their purpose in hopes of avoiding the actual assignments.

Remember to be excited about what you are going to teach your students. If you are not excited or act as if it is boring, your students will probably feel the same way. Students are intuitive and will know if you are not sincere. But if you are excited, they will pick up on this and be interested to learn why you feel this new lesson is exciting.

Whatever problems you have at home or outside the classroom have to be put on the back burner. You have to be a professional and move forward by thinking about your students and what they will learn that day. While students are in your classroom, you need to focus on meeting their academic needs. Any issues in your personal life need to be set aside. If that's not possible, you need to take a day off from teaching. This happens to everyone, so don't feel bad or embarrassed if you occasionally need a personal day.

Remember your audience. You have to be aware of everyone in the room and make sure you have everyone's attention before you start speaking. Take note of students who seem to be having an off day. If you can't get everyone to focus, you will be spinning your wheels, and everyone will get frustrated. You may need to pull students who are having an off day aside and talk to them before you start the lesson. This special one-on-one attention will very likely get their head in the game.

I know this seems like a lot to do before you even start your lesson, but as you get more experienced, this will become easier and easier. You will start doing these things out of habit and they will become second nature. Each day you may feel a little nervous until you get used to being at the front of the room. The more you get to know your students, the more comfortable you will feel. It can help to remember that you have prepared for this lesson and have all your materials organized.

Meeting Your Students for the First Time

Make a list of all the things you have to say to the students, so you don't forget anything. First, you and your students need to get to know each other in order to build a rapport. This rapport will help all of you to develop a level of trust. Begin by introducing yourself, giving the students some background on yourself and your goals for the year. You can mention your favorite hobby or food as a way to make a personal connection. Next, have each student introduce themselves. Ask them how many brothers or sisters they have so you can get to know them better. Ask them to share their favorite food to eat or a hobby of theirs. As they are talking, you will have time to relax and let the butterflies settle while you get to know your students better.

Once you have gotten to know your students a little, you are ready to move on to the items that need to be done on the first day. Review school policies and classroom rules, including consequences and rewards. This is the time to pass out any forms that need to go home for parent signatures. As you talk, you will start getting in your groove.

Once all your administrative information is given, you will be ready to start your lesson.

Don't forget to leave the last five minutes of class for reminders of what you need the students to do at home and what they need to bring back to class. Have them look around their desks and pick up any trash they see. These are good habits to end every class.

....

In this chapter, you learned about:

- Setting up your student roster
- Decorating your classroom
- Developing a behavior plan
- Planning your subjects
- Setting up class routines
- Learning emergency drills
- Prioritizing: the importance of a to-do list
- Knowing your colleagues
- Standing up at the front of the classroom
- Meeting your students for the first time
- Working smart

....

CHAPTER TWO
Foundations of a Good Classroom

There are pillars that make up the foundation of any good classroom. Professionalism is key to setting the tone. It's the first layer of bedrock to a solid classroom and a good relationship with your students, parents, colleagues, and really the whole community. It's important to have some best practices in place so you'll always know what to do when problems come up, when you have a student with disabilities, when you have to have a substitute come in, when you're thinking of spending your own money on supplies, and more.

Professionalism

Being professional is foundational to being a good teacher, and it doesn't need to be hard. With a little forethought, it's easy to be absolutely professional without adding stress to your day. In fact, knowing you've taken a few simple measures to show what a pro you are will actually cut down on your stress. On the other hand, thoughtless behavior and a lack of planning can have a negative impact on your career.

Be on Time

My husband always has a saying that if you aren't fifteen minutes early, then you are late. Punctuality is a must. It is vital to be on time for teaching and whenever you are expected at any type of function. This is a sign of respect for other people and yourself. When you are late, you are sending a message that you are more important than other people and that their feelings are not important. "I'm never on time!" is no excuse.

Leave home early enough to give yourself a ten-minute buffer in case there is a traffic accident or you have car problems. By arriving early, you are prepared in case there are any issues that have to be dealt with before you can start teaching. The copy machine that you usually use may be broken and you have to find another one to use. Or the technology you planned to use is not connecting right and you need a network person to help you fix the problem. Or materials you were going to use ended up breaking or getting messed up before you could use them. Issues like these are always popping up, but they're easily managed if you leave yourself a little extra time to handle them and still be ready by the time your class starts. By being early, you aren't rushing around and can be calm and composed when you start teaching. If the students are watching you rush to put away your belongings as they wait for you to start, you're setting a bad example for them!

Attendance

Of course, every teacher has unexpected problems come up or gets sick from time to time, meaning they need to miss school, but this should be a rare event. It is more trouble to be absent than it is to be in school. Plain and simple. Being absent means you have to create lesson plans for the substitute, make sure all of the students have their individual needs met while you are out, and any administrative duties you have are covered. Don't leave the school in a bind where they don't have any of this covered because this will make you look very irresponsible.

Dress for Success

Dressing appropriately is another must. You want to have students respect you, and one simple way to quickly command respect is to dress in business attire. School is a place of business and should be taken seriously. If you wear casual clothes, students will see school as a place to play and not work. Of course, there may be occasions to wear special clothes, but those should happen rarely and only with administrative approval. Most schools have a dress code for teachers, so if it isn't written in a handbook, ask an administrator.

Around the Holidays

When I first started teaching, our district had a rule that you couldn't be absent from work the day before or after a holiday without having a doctor's note. You should check with your district about this policy (and their general attendance policy). Even if it isn't a policy, it is a good habit to stick to. Usually, these days are very hard on students, staff, and faculty. You are going to have people who will take these days off and let the others pull their weight. Don't be one of those people. Be the teacher that your administration can depend on and they will remember when it counts.

Before a holiday, students are excited about the holiday and their behavior may be more erratic than usual, so having a substitute teacher can only add to the havoc. Likely you will have substitute plans that are more busy work than new material, and this only means the students have lost valuable learning time. If you are present, you can turn a holiday activity into a more meaningful experience than a substitute can. This stability is also important to many of your students because, during the holiday season, their home life might involve confusion or chaos rather than stability.

Off the Clock

Sometimes being a teacher may feel like living in a goldfish bowl. When you are out in the community, people may watch you, knowing you are a teacher. As a teacher, you are a leader in the community, so if you act inappropriately, it will be noticed. Most school districts will fire you if you are convicted of a crime of any sort. Driving under the influence of drugs or alcohol, shoplifting, or any other crime of moral turpitude could be grounds for dismissal if convicted.

It is good to get involved in local activities. Students and parents love to see teachers in the community. Students are always surprised that teachers have a life outside of the classroom because they are not used to seeing them in a different environment. When students see you at a store or a ballgame, they will mention it to their friends because they suddenly learn that you are a real person outside of the classroom. I've had students invite me to their community ball games or church festivals because they want to show off to their family and friends that their teacher cares about them. If you have a little time, it will be well worth it to attend these activities even if you can't stay for the whole time.

Documentation

Document all your communications during the school year. This includes communication between you and the administration, staff, colleagues, parents, and students. Keeping these records is good in case you have to refer back to the information at a later date. Also, it is a good way to show that you are keeping the lines of communication open between yourself and the parents. These kinds of communications can help you in your teacher evaluations.

Keep any emails sent to you or ones you replied to, letters from the district, handwritten notes from parents and colleagues. You can organize your emails on your computer and keep a physical file for all the other paperwork. Hold these at least through the first nine weeks of the next school year because you never know when a student's new teacher is going to have a question about the previous year. Or if you have instruction on a special procedure and someone asks you why you are doing things a certain way, you will be able to show the district or administrative letter instructing you to do this.

The Importance of Proofreading

Please make sure that any written material given to the students or sent home has been proofread. Nothing undermines your authority like misspelled words or poor grammar. You want to be the role model for your students and parents. Since you teach your students to proofread their work, you need to make sure that you do the same thing. If you hand out materials or forms that are full of mistakes, you are sending the message that you don't respect the recipients enough to take the time to make sure your letter is written correctly. If you are going to cut and paste information into a letter to a parent, make sure that you used the right student's name in your letter. I have gotten letters from my daughter's teacher with the wrong child's name on them. This made me wonder if I got the wrong letter or if the teacher was really knowledgeable about her information.

Professional Development

During the year, you may be expected to attend professional development sessions. Even if you don't think it applies to your teaching situation, it may apply in the future. So keep an open mind when you are there. Try to find ways that you can apply what you're learning to fit your teaching situation. Discussing the topic with colleagues and administrators can be helpful for this.

Every state requires you to take courses or have professional development credit in order to renew your teaching license. If your school or district offers free professional development courses, attend as many as possible. They may even earn you college credit for a nominal fee—better than paying full price at a local university. Check with your state department of education to find out how often you need to renew your license. Some of these courses may even apply toward getting an advanced degree in your subject area. I attended a lot of these courses in my district and was able to apply the credit to the renewal process and my master's degree. Years later, after checking into what courses I had taken and how much credit I had, I found out that I only needed one more course to get to a new level in the district's pay scale. You can never learn too much!

Remember that it is important that you are professional. You have put a lot of time and energy into your own education and training to get to this stage of your life. Hopefully, this will be a long-term career. Don't let any careless actions derail you from this! You want to be treated with respect and be seen as someone who takes education seriously.

Working with Administrators, Teachers, and Staff

In any job, you will run across colleagues and bosses you love and some that you don't get along with. Either way, you'll have to work with these folks every day, so it's worth putting in some effort to get along without giving in.

Dealing with the Administration

Remember that your boss is your employer and has the power to fire you. Even if you don't like what you are told to do, as long as it isn't illegal, you need to do it. You might explain to your boss why you disagree with them or why you would rather not do something, but make sure they know you will do it if they need you to do it. When these disagreements occur, remember not to speak poorly about your boss, your school, or your district with others because it will come back to haunt you. Do not bad-mouth your administrator or school ever! It is better to remember that if you have nothing nice to say, then say nothing at all. You often don't know who you are talking to or whether someone who may relay your words back to your supervisors is listening. Having respect for others will bring you more respect.

Extra Duties

Many times, teachers like to say that being assigned a specific duty (for example, extracurricular activities, bus duty, lunch duty, detention) isn't what they signed on to do in their contract, but usually most teaching contracts have a clause in it that states you may have duties other than teaching. You may have certain assigned duties that could be a pain, but you are still required to do them. If you have a conflict, you can ask an administrator if you can trade off with someone else or explain what your conflict is in hopes that it can be worked out. The worst thing to do is to ignore the duty and not show up.

Going Above and Beyond

Administrators are human too, and one way to make life easier is to get along with them as much as possible. Try to anticipate what they may need. If you know that a report on student enrollment is coming, ask what information will be needed and have that information on hand before it is asked for. Make sure you turn in what is requested on time or even early. Showing up to work early or offering to help when you see a need will get you brownie points with administrators.

Getting Told No

Remember that sometimes when you ask for permission to do something, your administrator may tell you no. Don't take this personally. The administrator is responsible for the whole school and must look at the big picture. Sometimes decisions have to be made in certain ways because it will affect the whole school. Sometimes your request may not be the best use of resources for the whole school. Funding may also be allocated to be used only in a certain way, so even though it will look like there is money for what you want, it may not be available for your needs.

Saying No

When you are first starting out in your career, it is really hard to say no when asked to do extra things. You want the administration to like you and you want your colleagues to see you as a team player. That is an easy way to quickly become overwhelmed by your job.

You need to learn to accept your limitations and say no. You can tell the principal that you appreciated his belief in your abilities but you really want to focus on being a good teacher. Unless you are assigned by him to do extracurricular activities (they don't usually like to make someone do something they don't want to do), you would prefer not to have that extra responsibility at this time. Maybe after you feel more confident in your teaching, you'd be glad to reconsider, but right now it is important that you focus on being an effective teacher. Usually the administration won't argue about that.

Stress Is Bad for Your Health—Really!

When I first started teaching high school, I was asked to be in charge of organizing the prom. I had only taught in elementary school and had no idea how to organize a prom, but of course I wanted the job, so I said yes. I was also asked to help with the cheerleaders, so of course I said yes. Not to mention learning all of the new high school procedures and expectations, which were very different from elementary school. It was an extremely stressful year. I spent every afternoon helping with cheerleader practice and then one night a week at football games and two nights a week at basketball games. Plus, I was skipping lunches to get my work done, and all my weekends were spent doing work too. Your body will react to stress whether you like it or not. You might not even realize you are under stress until your body lets you know. I've heard some people get migraines or intestinal troubles, but my body reacted by shedding all of my hair! What a shock. After two thousand dollars' worth of tests, I was finally told that it was due to stress.

Other Teachers

Concentrate on your own behavior and teaching skills. It's sad but true that teachers can pick up childish behaviors from their students and complain about other teachers who are leaving early or not doing what they should be doing. You never know if these teachers have gotten prior permission from the administration and you will sound like a child who is tattling on your colleagues, which is definitely unprofessional. These observations are the responsibility of the administration and not those of other teachers. As long you keep your focus on your own actions, you will do a better job because you won't waste time or energy on worrying about what other teachers were doing.

You don't have to like all of your colleagues, but you do have to respect them and treat them civilly. You might have a difference of opinion on politics or other issues, but don't let that keep you from being professional. If someone's ideas and opinions bother you, walk away. It doesn't help your situation to have a conflict with them—that will only add stress to your day.

If you do have a conflict with a colleague, try to sit down with them and discuss it. Make sure you don't put them on the defensive. Start by talking about how you are feeling and why. Make sure you listen to their side of the story and don't just focus on your side. Try to bring in some possible solutions to deal with this problem. If you can't solve the problem with your colleague, it is time to talk to an administrator—but don't escalate until you have tried to solve the problem between the two of you first.

Staff

Remember to get to know your school secretary and plant engineer. Even though your administrator is the boss, these two positions are usually the backbone to running things behind the scenes. The school secretary can make your life easy or hard at school. Most forms and requests to the administrator will route through this person. Your supplies may also come from this person. When you need information or help with school procedures, this person is the best resource to tell you how to do what needs to be done.

The plant engineer will help you if your heat or air-conditioning isn't working or if you need extra desks or chairs. The plant engineer makes sure the facility is working properly, and if you ever have problems with your classroom or need furniture for your room, this is the person you want on your side. Being friendly and collegial with these people is often your secret weapon for getting all the best stuff for your class!

Best Practices

There are a few rules for yourself and your classroom that you can have in place to make sure things run smoothly and you don't run into any unnecessary difficulties.

Constant Supervision

Never leave your class unattended. If you need to use the restroom or go to the office, always ask a colleague to watch your class. You should arrive in your classroom before any of your students do, and if you are not in it, your door should be locked so students may not enter it without an adult in the room. While there is no adult in the room, students may have a fight, or someone could be bullied. There have even been reports of sexual assaults during a time that the teacher has left the classroom. When any kind of incident occurs, parents will want to know where you were when it happened. If something happens and you have left the class without supervision, you will be the one liable.

Suspected Cases of Abuse

Any instances of abuse or suspected abuse need to be reported immediately to an administrator. Your school will have specific guidelines for this. If you don't report an allegation, you are breaking the law. It is not your job to investigate the allegations or determine if they are true or false before reporting it. Once you are made aware of possible abuse, you need to take action immediately. Many times a student is taking a risk by trusting you enough to share their scary situation with you—often hoping that you will help them. It's a good thing that all allegations are taken seriously because victims of abuse need to be heard and supported.

Excessive absences can also be a sign of something wrong at home. If you feel that a student has excessive absences, you should report it to the person in charge of attendance. Your school or district may have someone who will go out to check on the student to find out why there are so many absences. I had a student who was missing too many days of school. A social worker was sent to check on the student, and it turned out that that the student's mother had a substance abuse problem and was unable to drive her daughter to school when she missed the bus. Not long after that, the student was moved into a foster home and her school attendance and grades improved drastically.

Open-Door Policy

Never put yourself in a position where you are alone with a child in a closed space. If you have a student for detention after school, you should always leave the classroom door open. Sometimes you might team up with another teacher and put your detention students together while you monitor them together. If you have a conference with a student, you should never close the door of an office or meet with them alone. You should never drive a student home alone in your car. Not only is this improper, but if you got into an accident you could be liable. These behaviors help to ensure that students remain safe with teachers and help to protect you from any appearance of impropriety.

Accommodating Students with Disabilities

Besides students with different learning styles, you may have some students with disabilities in your class. It is important to identify if they have an individual education plan (IEP), and what accommodations and modifications you need to make for this student as required by law. Many teachers are resistant to making accommodations and modifications. They feel that these accommodations take a lot of the teacher's time away from other students, or they may object to the idea of giving the student any accommodations. Regardless of how you feel, you are required by law to provide the accommodations.

It is also a good idea to check with the student privately to see if they need anything. I have had some students tell me that I was the only person ever to ask them this. I don't think other teachers meant to ignore them but rather felt uncomfortable and didn't know how to address the disability. They were afraid to bring notice to it or felt like they might say the wrong thing. Teachers don't want to embarrass students, so they sometimes don't address what the student may need if it isn't written in the IEP. Students with disabilities may feel ignored because of this. I think it is important to address the elephant in the room and as long as you talk privately with the student, it is okay. In fact, many feel relieved that you care and ask them what they need. Many students don't know how to be a self-advocate, and this is a good way to help them learn.

Some of them are afraid to ask, so if you take the first step, this helps them begin. Encourage them to tell you what they need and know that sometimes it may not be possible, but it never hurts to ask.

Sometimes the accommodations you make for one student will be beneficial for the whole class. I had a student with autism who needed a visual schedule of the day. I realized that many of my students without disabilities benefited from the visual schedule. Making visual checklists for all of my students helped everyone stay focused and I was getting more completed work turned in on time.

I'll share more specific strategies in chapter seven, where I will talk about students with different disabilities and example strategies to use in your classrooms.

Substitute Plans

It is good to have a three-ring binder set up for your substitute plans and leave it close to your desk. If you know in advance that you will be absent, and you know your substitute, you can invite that person to your class beforehand to meet your students and show them your substitute binder. If this isn't possible, you can tell a colleague nearby where this binder is located so they can make sure that the substitute can find it. You can also tell students where this binder is and explain to the class that if you are ever absent, you expect good behavior and for them to make you proud of them. Let them know that you trust them to help the substitute with your routines and to not take advantage of the substitute. Once you tell them this, they are usually more cooperative because they don't want to hurt the trust you have in them.

In the first section should be your roster, which is updated every time your roster changes. You should also include your seating chart, classroom rules, and any other general information such as what you specifically lend to students and what you do not lend them. Also, give the location of any supplies that the substitute might need.

Then you should have a separate section for each class or subject that you teach. In this section, you can include your class routine that is followed every day. Here is where the lesson plan for that class is located, including any worksheets and location of materials that might be needed. By keeping a plastic sleeve here, turned-in papers can be inserted so you can easily find them when you return. You can also leave a blank sheet of paper labeled "Classroom Notes from Substitute" for the substitute to write you notes of specific things that might have occurred in the classroom if you need to know anything.

I have heard from many substitutes that they really appreciated this notebook and how much it helped them with the class. When a teacher is absent, it disrupts the normal routine that students are used to and can be chaotic for the substitute. I encourage them to leave me notes of not only the ones who misbehaved but also the ones who stepped up and worked harder than expected. I let the students know that I will be reviewing these notes when I return and if there are no reports of misbehavior, everyone will get a bonus reward.

Supply and Equipment Money

Before you start buying supplies, check with the school secretary to see what basic supplies the school gives you. Then check with your department head to find out what supplies and materials you can have from your department. There also may be some department money set aside for things, so you need to find out what is required in order to use that money. Sometimes you are only allowed to order from specific vendors, and there may be deadlines to turn in your requests.

If you find that you want to get things for your classroom that aren't available through the school, you can pay out of pocket for them. But be careful that you don't spend more of your own money than you can afford. Unless you are specifically told that you will be rimbursed, you need to consider it a donation to your class. There may be some teachers who can afford to spend a lot of their own money and some that can't. Usually, new teachers cannot afford to spend a lot of their own money for classroom extras and they shouldn't feel bad about this.

Some states give a stipend to teachers for supplies and equipment. Either your department head or administrator may help you find out how to get this money. Most of the time you need to buy things and turn in your receipts, but there may be a different process depending on where you live or teach. There may also be stipulations on what to buy and where to buy it.

There are online sites such as Donorschoose.org or GoFundMe.com where you can set up a fundraiser. You explain your project and specify how much money or materials you need. People can go to those pages and can donate money to help fund your project.

Sometimes you can ask parents for help obtaining something in particular. Parents may work at companies willing to donate materials or equipment. Parents might also have great suggestions on where you can get the materials cheaper than a regular store.

Getting Grants

There are also grants that are out there, but you have to hunt for them. Your district office might have someone specifically assigned to writing grants and may be able to help you learn about available grants. There are many grants that no one has even applied for and the money just sits there unused. Over the years I have written several grants and was given money for class projects that turned out worth the time and effort. You should check with your administration to see who you would contact in your district who would be able to direct you to specific grants for your class project.

One year I decided that I wanted my students to do landscaping around the school. I was able to describe the project, show how the project involves skills across many curriculums and would not only benefit my class but the whole school. Many times grant reviewers look at how the money can benefit the most people, so always try to show how this can help more than just your class.

I was able to apply again for several years after in order to build on my original project. Not only did we buy equipment and supplies for landscaping, but we were able to buy a storage shed to put it all in. My students were so proud of their project and were the stars of the school when the bushes and trees we planted were blooming.

If you find a grant that you are interested in applying for, make sure you follow the directions exactly. Many grants are denied because the applicant didn't follow the directions. Sometimes your district may even have a copy of a grant that was approved to use as a reference. After you are finished writing yours, try to sit down with someone with grant-writing experience to look it over before submitting it. This will help improve your chances of getting the grant approved.

In this chapter, you learned about:
- Being on time and coming to work every day
- Dressing for success
- Presenting yourself to the community even when you're off the clock
- Documenting all communications
- Proofreading everything you send home
- Taking advantage of professional development
- Working well with your administration
- Having a good relationship with your fellow teachers
- Understanding and working with school staff
- Making sure there is constant supervision in your classroom
- Handling it when you suspect or are told about abuse
- Keeping an open-door policy
- Accommodating students with disabilities
- Making plans for substitutes
- Spending money on supplies and equipment

CHAPTER THREE
Class Management

Class management is the key to effective instruction. Class management means that you have your class behaving appropriately in order to teach most effectively. Once your class knows what behavior you expect, they can act accordingly without direction or argument about their behavior. Without classroom management, you will spend more of your time with discipline than is necessary. This takes away from your classroom instruction time and your students won't learn as much as they should during class time. Once you get classroom management in place, it becomes second nature and you can spend your energy on classroom instruction.

Behavior Plans

The easiest and most effective way to manage your classroom is to have a clearly established behavior plan in place right from the get-go. It is worth the time and energy up front to make sure the students really understand your behavior plan. Too many times teachers skim over this part and want to jump right into their content material and that is why they struggle with their behavior plan.

Just like when you learn to drive, you have to learn the rules and take a written test before you are ever allowed behind the wheel of a car. The same should work in the classroom. For at least a week, you should review the program at the beginning of each class. This helps everyone develop a routine and shows the class how important this is to you. Students may roll their eyes and dislike that you keep going over the program, but don't let that stop you from continuing your process. Once you feel that everyone really understands the program, you can stop reviewing it.

Building Your Behavior Plan

Behavior plans should not be too complicated, or they will be hard to follow and enforce. In fact, five basic rules are all you need. The big ones are:

1. Be on time
2. Follow directions
3. Respect others
4. Come to class prepared
5. Complete assignments

You should think about the consequences of not following these behaviors, so you will have rewards and punishments ready to go. I laugh when I hear people say that a behavior plan shouldn't have punishments and that the teacher should only be positive. You want your students to be ready for real-life situations. When people speed and get stopped by police, they might get a ticket, have to go to court and get fined or go to jail as punishment. If you don't show up on time for your job or do what your boss asks you to do, you might get fired. On the other hand, if you do what is expected, you get a paycheck and may even get a bonus as a reward.

One thing that I've found successful for many years is that I don't present the plan to my students as a behavior plan. Instead, I present it to them as a job description and use a "token economy" system. Their role in my class is as a student. I share the behavior plan as their job duties. Rewards are listed as job benefits and punishments are listed as penalties. I give my students a mock salary with play money, and penalties were fines while benefits were extra pay. They could spend their money on rewards, which varied depending on the age of the child. Some rewards for younger children may be stickers, toys from the treasure box, candy, or happygrams (a positive note or picture about the student) sent home. Older students may prefer free time, library passes, or computer time. Eating and drinking in the class is usually prohibited schoolwide, so I sometimes used this as an expensive privilege for students to earn in my class.

Here is an example of my plan that worked in my classroom:

JOB TITLE: Student

JOB OBJECTIVE: To learn the necessary skills in order to be successful in today's world

JOB DUTIES:
1. Attend class
2. Be on time
3. Follow directions
4. Respect other people
5. Complete homework on time
6. Bring necessary materials to class

SALARY:
Each class attended: $10

PENALTIES:
$10 Disrespectful to others (each time)—
    write "Respect" paragraph
$5 1st offense—warning, initials on board
$10 2nd offense—check by initials, parent contact
$15 3rd offense—check by initials, lunch detention
$20 4th offense—circle around initials, parent contact
                        from the administration, and
                        after-school detention
$50 5th offense—referral to the office

*severe behavior will result in immediate referral to the office

If students don't come to class with their required materials, I let them rent a pencil or pen using the money they have earned, but I make them give collateral such as their student ID. This ensures that they return what they have borrowed. Penalties usually result in a loss of money because most students love the concept of money! I have found the loss of money is more effective than taking away any privileges that they might have. I kept an accounting sheet where students could save the money they accumulated each week and it would roll over to the next week.

Student's Name: _____
Date: _____

Accounting Sheet

	1st Period			2nd Period			3rd Period			4th Period			5th Period		
	add	sub	Tot	add	sub	Tot	add	sub	Tot	add	sub	Tot	add	sub	Tot
Monday - M															
Tuesday - T															
Wednesday - W															
Thursday - R															
Friday - F															
Weekly Balance															
Previous Week															
New Balance															
Penalties															
Not following directions ($5)															
Referral ($10)															
Benefits															
Break ($20)															
Library ($50)															
Computer ($100)															
Rent materials ($5)															
Paper ($1)															
Pencil ($20)															
HW pass ($100)															
Eating/Drinking ($200)															

Once you develop a plan, run it by your administrator to make sure you have their support. If there is anything that they won't support, you need to revise your behavior plan. This is important because if there is an issue in the future and a parent comes to a conference, you want to make sure that the administration is prepared to support you. Once you establish a plan, send it home to be signed by the students and the parents and keep a copy of it in the student's file. Post a large poster of the plan along with rewards and consequences on the wall in the classroom so it is visible all year long.

Take the Time, Make Adjustments

Of course, this is going to take time to set up and explain to students and parents, but it is well worth the effort once everyone gets used to it. It may take a month before it becomes second nature, but the most important thing is to be consistent and fair. Students are very observant, and if you aren't fair or consistent, your behavior plan will never work.

The most important thing is that you find a plan that works for you and your students. If you try to fit a behavior plan into your day but you know that this doesn't fit your teaching style, it just won't work for you. You may find a token economy plan too cumbersome to keep up with and need something easier. I'm a big token economy fan, so this plan worked well for me for thirty years, but there are lots of other options. You could make a chart with the student's names on it with red, yellow, and green Post-it notes beside each name. When a student doesn't follow the rules, you take off the green note and continue until the red note. Or you could give plastic chips when they are acting appropriately and take them back when they're not. I know one teacher who gave each student an index card with their name on it and went around with a hole puncher each time the students were acting appropriately. Some teachers have made behavior contracts with specific rewards listed just for individual students.

If you try a plan, stick with it for at least a month. It takes that long for everyone to get used to a new system, and you won't see many positive results until then. I have seen too many teachers try a behavior plan for a week and then scrap it because it wasn't working. I don't believe they gave the plan enough time to really judge if it was working or not. Of course, you might have to adjust the plan a little, but no major changes to it should happen for at least a month. You might decide to adjust the reward and penalty amounts in order to motivate the students to behave appropriately more often. Maybe the reward is not motivating enough. After a month, if it isn't working, try something new.

Tactics for Creating a Positive Classroom Environment

Now that you have your behavior plan, it's time to think about managing the students in your classroom on the day-to-day. Sometimes small strategies can have large impacts, especially when it comes to creating a positive atmosphere.

Don't Forget to Laugh and Breathe

Remember to have a sense of humor. It is important to be fair and consistent, but some instances can be controlled with a good sense of humor. I don't mean that you should laugh at them or their mistakes, but deflecting with some humor can easily de-escalate some situations. For instance, if you feel yourself getting worked up, try to stop to take a deep breath. If you realize that you are overreacting, just grin at the student and say, "I'm acting silly, aren't I? I'm sorry." This usually surprises the student and gives everyone a chance to calm down. Some things just aren't worth the battle, and you really need to pick what battles you are willing to fight.

Getting the Students' Attention

An important behavior that you want your class to learn is the cue that tells them to stop talking and focus on you. This really helps when you are ready to transition to a new lesson or activity and you don't want to waste precious minutes trying to get everyone to be quiet and to listen to your instructions. Different teachers use different techniques. Some flick the light switch on and off, which is great except when you are somewhere there is no light switch. Some teachers raise their hand in the air and have the students copy this action and stop talking when they see it. Some teachers use a phrase to get everyone's attention. Some teachers clap their hands until the whole class is clapping in time with the teacher. It is best that you find the cue that works for you and use it consistently.

Use Incentives

Throughout my own school career, good grades were important to me and getting an A was extremely rewarding. I was crushed whenever I got any grade lower than a B. So, when I first started teaching, I felt discouraged when my students weren't studying for their tests and many were failing. I decided that I would give them an incentive to do better and I told them that we would play a game to help them study. If they got the right answer they would get a "point," and for every five points, their test grade would go up a point. I was so excited to give them this extra help to get a better grade but was truly disappointed when no one else was as excited as I was. We played the game and hardly anyone knew the answers because they still did not study. When I discussed this with my boyfriend at the time (who later became my husband), he told me that my incentive would not have worked for him at all. As a student, he would not have cared about getting extra points or getting good grades because they didn't mean anything to him. Instead, he would have wanted a reward that meant something to him, not to me. As an experiment, we went out and bought a huge bag of Tootsie Rolls. During class, if the student got the right answer, they got a piece of candy. Soon, all of the students were studying so they could earn that piece of candy. I was amazed at how my rewards were so different from what their rewards were! Now, I don't advocate giving candy to students, and in some schools this is not even allowed anymore. Instead, I start out giving the students a survey to see what rewards are important to them.

Using a checklist, you could suggest things such as happygrams, a pencil, an eraser, fifteen minutes of computer time, a library pass, a phone call home, fifteen minutes of free time, fifteen minutes of drawing time, or fifteen minutes of listening to music with headphones. You can create a list of things that you are willing to give, but leave a spot for them to write their own rewards. This helps you know what will be meaningful to them and not you. Rewards work to motivate those students who are not following directions when given, talking without raising their hands, not completing classwork or homework, not staying in their seats, and disrupting the class. Make sure that you are not rewarding bad behavior, only good behavior. This may mean ignoring the bad behavior and looking really hard for good behaviors. It is important when giving the rewards that you specify the good behavior that you are rewarding.

Give Positive Support

Another simple thing I did in our class was to use positive support. I think it is easy for everyone to fall into a pool of negativity and it is hard to get out of that bad habit. When my students accomplished something, or someone got a good grade, we applauded their success. If someone said something negative, we stopped and talked about it. We discussed how we could change that negative talk into positive talk. Eventually, I did this less and less because students behaved differently toward each other. There was more encouragement and support rather than putting one another down. At first I worried that they were just being more positive in my class so they wouldn't have to discuss negative and positive talk. Then I noticed that this behavior was carrying on outside of class, so I felt they were applying these skills.

Slowly my students' grades were improving. As they started to feel better about themselves, they were feeling more confident. More class-work assignments were being completed. When they made mistakes, it wasn't the end of the world and it didn't mean that they were dumb. My students knew that if they tried their best and they made mistakes, they just needed to dust themselves off and learn from their mistakes. They also knew that when they didn't try their best, they deserved the grade they got. Soon students were helping and encouraging one another not to feel bad.

After some time had passed, some of the parents noticed that their child seemed happier and more confident at home and in school. I had explained some of the positive-behavior techniques we were using in class and how I hoped it would improve their academic abilities too. Parents were very supportive of this.

Teach Them to Give and Receive Compliments

A lot of students seem to learn that negative interactions are easier than positive ones. It is easier and funnier for them to insult others and put them down instead of complimenting and building them up. Many students are greatly affected by their peers' positive statements about them. For this activity, first we brainstorm positive words that describe others. I write these on the board to help students who may have trouble with spelling. Then I give everyone a piece of construction paper with their name at the top of the paper in Magic Marker. When I give the signal, everyone passes their paper to the person in front of them. The end of each row will pass this to the person on their left. Everyone has two minutes to write a positive word they think describes the person who is listed at the top of the page. Then they move the paper to the next person. When the paper eventually returns to the original person, we stop and I share some of the papers. I love to see the faces on my students as they read the words that their classmates have written down about them. I collect all of the papers and laminate them before returning them to the students. Some of the students told me that their parents had this framed and hung in their room at home.

Make It Easy to Ask for Help

I learned this great behavior strategy when I was eating at a restaurant. On the table they had two miniature license plates—one was green and one was red. If you turned them so that the red was showing, any server would stop to see what you needed. If it was green, they left you alone to enjoy your meal in peace. I thought this would be a great tool to use with my students. I cut red and green foam panels into thee-inch-by-three-inch squares. Then I glued one red square to a green square. On the red square, I wrote the word "Help" in big letters, and on the green square I wrote the word "Okay" in big letters. These were kept on the corner of every student's desk. When the students arrived, it was turned over so that the green side was showing. While doing their work at their seats, the students turned it over to the red side whenever they needed help. This eliminated the need for students to keep their hands raised hoping to get the teacher's attention. After helping a student, I was able to turn their square back to green and then scan the desks to see who else needed my help.

TEACHING SOCIAL SKILLS

All students of every age need some instruction in social skills.

Spend a little time talking about manners, such as saying please, thank you, I'm sorry, and excuse me. These are little things, but they can have a huge impact on others. You can also talk about table manners, such as using a napkin and not chewing with your mouth open. It surprises me how many students do this when I am walking through the cafeteria!

For the bigger social skills lessons, I like to use G-rated movies with a moral to the story. I have used the old Disney movie *Dumbo* to teach students not to give up and to believe in their abilities. I like showing *Finding Nemo* to teach students that everyone is different and we should never underestimate what we can do. For older students, I like to show *The Blind Side*, *Grace Unplugged*, or *Soul Surfer*, which deal with overcoming obstacles and perseverance. There are a lot of movies that can be used to teach social skills. Just make sure you vet them thoroughly and they're approved by the administration before you show them.

Create Positive Peer Pressure

Another strategy I use is (gentle) peer pressure. Using my token economy system, I encourage my students to save money, and when everyone has two hundred dollars of play money in their account, we will do something fun as a class. Sometimes I have a pizza delivered or we watch a movie (approved by the administration). This usually happens only two or three times a year. When students see other class members not coming to class prepared or not doing their homework, which results in rental fees or loss of pay, they are quick to encourage them to do better.

This usually helps without making me the bad guy.

Another way to use positive peer pressure is a class paper chain that gets built from the ceiling to the floor. If I'm having a problem with a specific rule not being followed by different students, I will start making tally marks on the board. If there are no more than three tally marks on the board at the end of the class, the class earns a link that is added to the paper chain. When the chain reaches the floor, the whole class gets a reward. This visual of the tally marks and the chain help to remind students to follow the rules.

A Case for This Point

By getting to know your students and their behaviors, you may be able to notice when they are having a problem. They may not feel comfortable coming up to you about their problem but will feel relieved if you address it first. I found this out one day when I noticed my usual bubbly student seemed distracted and withdrawn. At first when I asked her about it, she told me she was just tired but she was fine. I kept a watchful eye on her and noticed that she seemed upset even if she was saying otherwise. I found time to meet with her again, and when I pressed the issue, I found out that she was pregnant and her parents didn't know. We went straight to the guidance counselor and worked out a plan for her to tell her parents. I was able to get her some help and her parents were very thankful that I was there.

Know Your Students

It is important to really get to know your students so that you are aware of any changes in their behavior and their work. Take time to greet your students at the door every day and shake their hand. It is amazing what you can learn about a student in this simple way. Some will look you in the eye and smile as they give you a firm handshake. Others may look at the floor and give you a weak handshake. Some may even get emotional at this simple act of attention that they don't get anywhere else. If you ask a student how they are or how their weekend went, really try to focus on their answer. Nothing is more hurtful than to hear a teacher ask this and then having their answer ignored as if they don't matter. When a teacher shows that they really care how a student is doing, they will feel like they matter and will work harder for their teacher.

Getting Students to Trust You

Earning your students' trust takes time—it won't happen overnight. You have to have faith that it will happen and when it does, everything will fall into place. Once it does, students will find learning more exciting and you will find teaching them easier too. This concept is important to share with the students. Explain that learning to trust each other is a two-way street and all of you need to do this in order for learning to be successful.

Students need to trust you in order to learn from you. For students, they are taking a big risk in order to learn new things. They might make a mistake and other students may make fun of them. They might fail and failure hurts. They feel very vulnerable when learning something new. Many want to please the teacher and are afraid of looking bad in front of you.

In order for students to really learn something new and retain their new learning, they have to trust their teacher. They have to trust that their teacher won't let others ridicule them. They trust that their teacher won't let them get hurt. They trust that the teacher will be there when needed. But how do you really get this message across?

I emphasize that honesty is important to me. I promise not to lie to students and ask that they respect me and be honest with me also. These might just seem like fancy words to them at first, but I make sure that when I promise to do something, I stick with my promise. When I'm honest with them, I also let them know that I'm being honest. Once this starts to sink in, you'll really see a difference in your classroom. I even ask students to share with me times when they have felt that a teacher has betrayed them and not been honest with them. I like to share times when I've felt betrayed when a student lied to me. This can be an enlightening experience for all.

I also tell my students that I will be there to help them. I tell them that this is my job, that I am there to make sure that they are not on this journey of learning alone. I will not tolerate others making fun of someone who is learning. I promise them that if they give their best effort and do everything in their power to succeed, I won't let them fail. But we both will know if they are doing their best. I promise that I will help them all that I can, and if I can't, I will help them find someone who can.

And I don't just tell them this at the beginning of the year. I tell them this often. I tell them this until they believe me and can tell that I'm sincere. I show them with my actions that they can believe what I'm saying.

It takes only one instance of betrayal to permanently lose a student's trust. Students will know if you are not sincere and they will know if you lie to them. It is important that you are honest with your students. If they ask you something personal that is private, don't lie to them but tell them this is personal and you don't want to talk about it. You don't owe them answers to inappropriate questions; you owe them the honest answer that the topic is off-limits. They will appreciate and respect you more for telling them this.

Finding the Real Dream
I had a friend who told me that his intellectually disabled student wanted to be a doctor. Rather than laugh at this dream or tell the student that the dream was impossible, the teacher questioned the student further. After long discussions, the teacher found out that the student really just wanted a job where he wore a white jacket like a doctor. So the teacher helped him explore jobs that had a uniform of a white jacket. One of them was working in a hospital cafeteria. After an internship in a hospital cafeteria, the student knew that this was his dream job!

Dreams Can Come True

It is important that you help your students dream and work toward making their dreams come true. Many students say they don't know what they want to be because many times they are told that they are not being realistic or that they are not capable. Nothing pops a dream bubble faster than negative thoughts. When a student tells you what their dream is, it is important to question them further to find out how you can help them.

When a student declares a dream that may seem unrealistic or unattainable, you need to do more investigation. Ask the student why he chose that dream. The answer may help you direct him to a different path that will still help him achieve his goal. If the student wants to be a pro athlete, he may want this because he wants to earn a lot of money. By looking at the student's strengths, you may help him move in a direction where playing to his strengths can eventually earn him money in the future. You sometimes have to play the detective and really investigate the motives behind the dream. Then you have to find the resources and opportunities that are possible for the student.

Overcoming Resistance

Many times students will be resistant to completing assignments, which is a natural response. Everyone has at one time or another procrastinated to avoid tasks they aren't thrilled about. Most people don't want to do something they think is hard or that they might fail. This can turn into a big power struggle between the students and the teacher. As a teacher, it is important for the students to know that you are more stubborn and can outlast them because you are older and have more practice. It's your job to get them to do their job. Also let them know that when they struggle with an assignment, you will be there to help them and they are not alone. In the same respect, you want them to see you as their teacher and not their friend. They may say they hate you or throw a tantrum, but that is okay as long as in the end they complete the assignment and learn the lesson. They already have many friends, but they don't have enough effective teachers in their lives. You don't have to be their friend. Some of the best teachers I remember were the ones who made me work hard and taught me many things. They were somewhat intimidating and had high expectations of me, and while I respected them and enjoyed being in their classes, they were never my friends.

Failures Are Opportunities to Do Better

Many of your students will have faced so many failures that they feel like a failure. It is worth taking the time to explain to them that their failures don't define them. It may take a while, but if you keep at it, the message will sink in. Then they can come to understand that failures are just opportunities to do better.

Even though I spend a lot of time convincing my students this, I forget that the same applies to myself. Many times your lessons won't go as planned. The students might not be as engaged in the lesson as you had wanted them to be. Sometimes you are really excited about a lesson and the students think it is boring. Other times you think the lesson may be difficult for the students and they may find it boring, but instead they find it fascinating. Maybe you had some technology issues or materials did not work. These things happen. You just need to make sure that you look at the reasons why the lesson didn't work so well and figure out how to keep this from happening next time.

If more lessons go wrong than right, that means you need to change something. Since you can only change your behavior, you need to evaluate your actions and how you are teaching. Focus on what has worked and how you can use those strategies in place of ones that aren't working. Remember that teaching is always a work in progress, and you haven't failed unless you give up.

High Expectations

Have high expectations for your students. Expect them to do well and push them to try harder. Don't help them make excuses not to do their best. By not expecting much of our students, we are reinforcing the self-fulfilling prophecy theory. We are saying that they are not smart enough or good enough to do what others expect from them.

Don't just accept the minimum that a student can do. Once the student reaches a level of success, it is time to move forward. Move the bar a little higher and help them reach that new goal. Once they reach that goal, move to a harder one. Always encourage them to try something a little more challenging than what they have already achieved. If they don't succeed at first, drop back to their last level of success. Allow them to succeed in some things you know they are capable of doing before encouraging them to try again to do something harder. Never give up on them and never let them give up.

High Expectations in Practice

The first time I had a student with Down syndrome in my class, I really didn't know how hard to push him. He was lovable and kind, but all I saw were his limitations, and he got away with a lot of things that I wouldn't allow my other students to get away with. I felt bad if he got upset when he couldn't do something, so I didn't give him a lot of assignments that confused him or that he struggled to do. I had no experience with students with this kind of disability, so I thought I was doing the right thing. Even the gym teacher was not pushing him to dress for PE because she thought he wasn't capable or that the other kids would bully him. Then we had a conference with his mother and shared with her some of the things he was not doing. She was shocked and quickly set us straight that he was more than capable of doing many of the things I should have had him doing. After talking with her, I agreed that if I had any doubts about his ability to do something, I needed to call her. Quickly, I was having the student do more complex things and he was doing them successfully in the classroom. In PE, he was dressing without a problem. This parent helped me learn that I needed to have higher expectations for all of my students. By expecting them to do the least I thought they could do, that is all that they would perform. Students are smarter than we think and they know when they are able to con the teacher!

Handling Stress

Everyone gets stressed. From test time to family issues to the problems of the world, there's a lot to worry about, and everyone—teachers and students—react to stress in different ways. In most cases, stress can lead to irritability, feeling run-down, becoming withdrawn, and maybe even some health issues. In more dire cases, people can resort to violence against themselves or others.

You may hear a lot of older people complain that kids today don't really know what stress is compared to older generations, but I find this to be faulty thinking. Students today face a different kind of stress, and it really doesn't matter what is causing their stress; it still is harmful to the students.

One way to help your students deal with stress is to encourage their hobbies. By showing interest in a student's hobbies, you are showing that you care about them. I had a student who competed in skateboard competitions and loved to show me the videos of his latest competition. I told him how worried I was about him getting injured but was excited that he had so much ability! This made him so proud and he actually worked harder in class for me. He felt like he mattered in my classroom.

You can help students learn to handle stress in your classroom. If you see only one or two students who are showing signs of stress, encourage them to put on headphones and listen to some calming music. Stress balls are cheap and easy to find. Hand these to a student to squeeze when they are feeling stressed. Or have them take a break from what they are doing and work on something else. If you see a lot of students stressing at the same time, stop working and take them for a walk or do some exercises in the classroom. Get out some fun music and start dancing! This will help get them into a better frame of mind when they return to their task.

Beating the Doldrums

Sometimes in the middle of the year, you and your class may get into the doldrums. Everything seems boring and nobody wants to do anything. The weather is dismal and dreary, which affects everyone's moods. The students don't want to do any work, and nothing seems to interest them. Even you find the normal routine boring.

Having the doldrums is natural in the middle of the year. If you fight it or deny it, you will only end up wasting time trying to get students to focus. The harder you try to get them engaged, the less they want to be motivated. It tends to be a losing battle. Instead, it is time to change the normal routine. Even though routines are wonderful, it is time to get out of the rut and break the cycle of boredom. You may do something different for one day or even a week. This might be a single lesson or a whole unit.

Think of ways to shake things up. Do something unexpected or unusual to introduce your lesson. You might dress up as a historical character or plan a little skit with another teacher to introduce the lesson. You might bring in a speaker or have them in on Skype.

Take time to read a fun and exciting short story for a few minutes each day. Ask students to predict what will happen next. Ask them why they think this will happen. Allow them to draw pictures of what happened in the part that you just read.

Have students make a scale model of the school using cardboard and Popsicle sticks. This will involve students measuring certain areas of the school and the class deciding what the scale will be. Have students get in groups to make different parts of the building. When all of the parts are put together, you will have a scale model that everyone will be proud of.

Depending on the weather and the time of year, take your class outside. If there is a sunny, bright day, it may be warm enough to take your class outside. Plan your lessons to include some outside activities. Have them observe their surroundings and ask them to point out things that have changed from last season or the last time your class was outside. Once someone starts pointing out the changes, the rest of the class will start looking for others so they can participate in announcing differences.

Take a break from the unit you are teaching to teach a mini lesson about something totally different. It can be a hands-on experiment for students to learn an exciting new concept. Or you can have learning centers set up about a specific topic. Make sure that all the students are able to move around.

After this single or unit lesson, return to your normal routine. You and the students will be in a better mood and have a better attitude toward this routine after a break.

....

In this chapter, you learned about:
- Creating and adjusting behavior plans
- Effecting a positive atmosphere in the classroom
- Using incentives and positive support to get the best from your students
- Teaching students about the importance of giving and receiving compliments
- Making it easy for students to ask for help
- Getting to know your students and gaining their trust so you can make sure they stay on track
- Identifying a student's dreams and showing them how to achieve them
- Overcoming a student's resistance to learning
- Turning failures into opportunities
- Getting great results through high expectations
- Dealing with stress
- Getting through the doldrums

....

CHAPTER FOUR
Dealing with Bad Behavior

Even if you do everything possible to set up a positive classroom environment, you will have to deal with bad behavior. Every teacher does. It's part of the job! It can be frustrating and even upsetting, but if you have a plan for identifying and dealing with issues ahead of time, you'll be in great shape to overcome even the most challenging confrontations. Here are some effective strategies I've used for spotting and dealing with problematic behaviors on the individual level as well as for motivating the whole class to do their best.

Identifying Bad Behavior

It is important to identify the problem behavior of individual students. You can't just say that you want the student's behavior to improve. First you have to decide which behavior you would like to change. Then it is important to determine what happens before this behavior occurs and what happens after. If you understand what is triggering a behavior, you might be able to take preventative action to keep it from happening. If you also learn what rewards the student gets from acting this way—such as getting attention or getting out of doing work—you might be able to change the rewards that encourage this inappropriate behavior. Sometimes students disrupt class because they are bored and are not being challenged. Others may disrupt the class because they don't understand what they are supposed to do and are afraid of looking "dumb." Nothing is worse for them than to have their peers think they are dumb! Once the student shows appropriate behavior, it is important that this is recognized and praised even if there is no extrinsic reward included.

WHAT IF YOU DON'T LIKE A STUDENT?

It is natural that you won't always like all of your students. There may be some students whose personalities rub you the wrong way and you can't feel the same for them as you may others. It is okay. Really! It's not a failure to not like every kid you ever teach. What you do need to do is remember that you are the professional and you need to look beyond these feelings and do your job. Your job is to help these students succeed by giving them tools and strategies to overcome any obstacles that may stand in their way.

If you're having trouble connecting with or liking a student, it can be helpful to develop some kind of rapport with them. Find out what they like to do when they aren't in school. What kind of hobbies do they have? Do they have any special talents that they are proud of and want to share? Getting to know these students may help you feel some connection with them. Over time you may realize that your initial feelings have changed as you get to know this student better.

If you are still having trouble understanding a student or connecting with him, check with other teachers and see how they are connecting with that student. Maybe they will have suggestions on something that you can do that would help you connect with him. Just as you work better with some students than others, some students also may prefer different teachers because they feel some kind of connection with them and not you. If you are working with a co-teacher, you may find your co-teacher has more success with certain kids than you do, and this is fine. In fact, it's great! Take advantage of it and allow that teacher to work with that student most of the time.

No matter what, just remember that you don't have to like your student to do your job effectively.

Physical Punishment

Never hit a child! This may seem obvious, but if you watch the news, it seems that some teachers get so frustrated, they forget this important rule. At no time is it ever appropriate to strike a student with your hand or any object. Teachers may get frustrated with a student, but if you get so frustrated that you want to hit a student, you need to remove yourself immediately from the situation. You need to get another teacher or administrator to supervise your class and you need to go somewhere to calm down.

Building Self-Esteem to Beat Bad Behavior

It may seem surprising, but a lot of bad behavior stems from self-esteem issues. Some students with low self-esteem may be withdrawn and have no confidence. Other students may bully their classmates in order to try to make themselves feel better. They want to appear stronger and tougher than their peers. Those with low self-esteem tend to refuse to try because they feel like failures, so why should they set themselves up to fail once more? Some of them may boast and brag that they know how to do just about everything so they don't have to show that they really don't know what you are talking about or how you want them to do something. Having negative thoughts about themselves only creates a self-fulfilling prophecy. If they think they can't do something or they aren't smart enough or good enough, they believe this about themselves and keep themselves from succeeding. As their teacher, you can play a big role in showing them their potential, which is wonderful in its own right, plus it will in cut down on problematic behavior.

Create Early Successes

Building up self-esteem can go a long way toward helping improve behaviors and lead to more effective teaching. If you aren't spending most of your time dealing with discipline problems, you will be able to teach more effectively. When you start giving assignments, make sure that the first few are assignments that your students can be successful with. You may have to prompt them to get the correct answers, but whatever you have to do without giving them the actual answer is going to be helpful in the big picture. I have had some students come up to me with their paper and ask me if I graded it right because they aren't used to getting so many answers correct. Once they start tasting success, it is easier for them to accept the mistakes they make. They don't think that their mistakes define them as failures.

ONLY HUMAN

I like to set a good example for my students. One way I do this is to explain that I'm only human and I sometimes have bad days like they do. I always kept two small stuffed animals in my classroom. One was a pink unicorn that I put out on my desk to show that I was in a good mood and having a good day. The other was an angry bull, and when I put that on the corner of my desk, it meant that I was not having a good day and I may not be as nice as I usually am. I might be grumpy and not in the mood to joke around. That was the time to treat me gently and not do things to aggravate me, because I might overreact in my bad mood. I rarely ever had to put the bull out, but if I ever did, usually the students were good as gold. Then one day a student came in and asked if he could borrow my bull because he was having a very bad day and just wanted everyone to leave him alone. I allowed him to do this, and no one bothered or teased him during class. After class I asked him if there was anything I could do to help him, and he said no, that having the bull on his desk gave him time alone to cool down and kept him from getting angrier.

Have a Class Motto

For a couple of years, I kept data on my students' self-esteem and how it affected their learning. At the beginning and at the end of the school year, I had students fill out a self-esteem rating scale. I also kept a chart showing whether their grades had improved or not. By the end of the year, I learned that grades improved when my students' self-esteem improved.

I decided that my students had experienced a lot of failures over time and some of them felt defeated. I needed to find a way to turn this negative thinking around. So I came up with a class motto. Our class motto was "I am a born winner!" By making it a regular part of our classroom life, I was able to help bolster the students' self-esteem. I explained to my students that no one was born to fail. It didn't matter what religion or culture they belonged to—they were born to succeed in life. By convincing themselves that they were not capable of doing something, they couldn't do it—not because they weren't capable, but because they didn't believe they could. I went over this every day for a week. Then I went over it at the beginning of every week for a month. Next it was every other week until I was talking about this only at the beginning of every month. The students needed this pep talk. They knew I was sincere, and they believed it. I think some of them wanted to believe it but were afraid to.

On every wall of my classroom, I hung a large poster with our class motto on it. I let the students decorate the posters. At the beginning and the end of each day, I asked the students what our class motto was. Whoever I asked got some small reward if it was answered correctly. On every paper they turned in for a grade, they needed to write our class motto at the top of their papers. At first students were reluctant to write the motto on their papers, but if it was turned in without the motto, I refused to accept it. Eventually this became a routine that they were comfortable with, and they continued to do it all year long. It is amazing that something this easy could make such an impact. I saw some of my students years later and they brought our class motto up in our conversation. One young lady went through a terrible divorce, but she had our class motto on a slip of paper in her wallet. Whenever she was feeling defeated, she looked at the paper and kept repeating the motto. Another young man became the pastor of a church and talks about our class motto in his sermons.

You can use my class motto as your own, or come up with one that resonates with you. No matter what it is, show your students that you are sincere about it and keep using it until they start to believe. They might be resistant to it at first and think it's cheesy, but if you work on it long enough, it will start to sink in.

Dealing with Conflict

One fear that many teachers have is knowing how to deal with conflicts. Being prepared to handle conflicts, which will happen eventually, will help you feel more comfortable when they occur. Knowing how you should act will help take your stress down a notch or two during the conflict.

Student Outbursts

When students have outbursts, remember to stay calm. Take a deep breath and don't overreact. It is important not to take student outbursts personally even though they may say hurtful words to you. Sometimes students have outbursts to test you and see if you will enforce the limits that you have set in the classroom. Other students are also watching to see how you handle the outbursts, and your actions will set the tone of the class from that point on.

Remember to be fair and consistent, so follow your behavior plan. Never resort to arguing with a student—it will only escalate the problem. It takes two people to have an argument. If you remove your response, they can't argue. Don't try to have the last word, because they will want to have the last word and then it becomes an argument.

There may be some reason that the student is angry, but trying to reason with a student while he is angry is never going to work. Acknowledge that you know the student is upset and that you want to help them calm down. Suggest that when he calms down, you might be able to help him, but you can't help him until you can have a calm conversation at a later time.

Talk calmly and softly to him, which sometimes will help him calm down. Let him know what rule you need him to follow. If he stops his outburst and follows the rules, immediately praise him and let him know how glad you are that he is following the rules.

If the outburst continues and you can't get the student to comply, it may be time to contact an administrator. Make sure that you use this as a last resort. If you are constantly calling the administrators to your classroom to help with discipline, you are showing them that you aren't able to control your own students.

Verbal Conflict

If two students start becoming angry and exchange words, try to get them as far away from each other as possible. This might mean that they have to sit in different areas of the room, or you might have to remove a student and ask another teacher to take him while he calms down in their classroom. Let everyone have a few moments to calm down before addressing the issue. Rather than overreacting and escalating the situation when students get into some sort of conflict, try to give them time to calm down before discussing it with them. It doesn't do any good to try to reason with a student who is angry.

Let each student have their say about what happened while you listen. Even though their reasoning may be faulty, let them talk without interrupting them. Sometimes it just helps for them to have their say and have someone listen to them. You might even rephrase what they say about how they are feeling and why. This will show them that you are sincere about hearing what they are saying. By actively listening, they don't think you are just letting them talk but not really listening to them. Help students find a way to compromise or settle this problem. Ask students to think about other ways they could have solved the problem without getting angry. Depending on their age, students can tell you their responses, write them out, or even draw them.

WHEN *YOU* GET UPSET

There will be times you get upset, but you will need to learn ways to stay calm no matter what. Do not lose control in front of your students. You want to be the role model that they follow especially when they get upset. If (and when! because it will happen) you get upset, you want to show your students how you handle this emotion. Sometimes your actions will speak louder than your words.

It is good to warn students if you are starting to get frustrated or annoyed. You want them to learn the material, and you may get frustrated if they don't understand it as quickly as you would like them to learn it, especially if you feel like they're just not putting in the effort. When this happens, take deep breaths and try to take a break so you can calm down. You can let your students know that this is happening and that your emotions have nothing to do with them, that the frustrations are your own. Having this talk is a great way to get students to understand that you get upset just like they do. And you make efforts to understand why you feel the way you do and to calm yourself down. This will go a long way in keeping their respect and in role modeling how they can deal with their own anger and frustrations.

One-on-one, students may annoy you when they don't follow directions or complete their tasks, but you should stay calm and objective when dealing with them. All of the students are watching you in order to see if you will be fair and consistent. Follow the steps of your behavior plan in order to help your student be more successful.

So that's how you deal outwardly with getting upset. But what about your own personal welfare? If you find that you're getting really upset and feel out of control, you might be overstressed and overreacting. A lot of times you will get easily upset when you are not drinking enough water, not eating regular healthy meals, not getting enough exercise, or not getting enough sleep.

When you feel yourself getting upset, try to be honest with yourself about what may be causing you to get upset and think of ways to change your habits. You may need to ask another teacher to watch your class while you leave and calm yourself down. Or you may even share with your class that you are upset with them and need a few minutes of quiet time, so you would appreciate it if they didn't talk to you for a few minutes. Students appreciate honesty and will respect your feelings more than if you try to disguise them.

It may help if you just vent your feelings and talk with another colleague. They may give you some insight and suggestions to why you are overreacting.

Even if you don't feel like doing it, try to get more exercise each day, even if it is just walking for thirty minutes. Getting regular exercise will help you have a better mental attitude and keep you from overreacting.

Make sure you are staying hydrated. If you get dehydrated, you will feel tired and out of sorts. This may make you feel depressed or angry. Staying hydrated will keep your energy levels up and help your mood.

When you are upset, remember that the only actions you can control are your own and not anyone else's. Ask yourself what changes you can make in your own actions that could help you feel better. You might choose to follow through with this or not, but at least you are allowing yourself to have options.

I ask them to describe what they did that got them in trouble. Then I ask them to write or tell about what they should have done. Sometimes writing or talking about the behavior helps to defuse the situation and lets them get their anger out in words. If they are writing or telling it into a recording device, they don't have to worry about someone interrupting them and not getting their voice heard. Writing about what they should have done helps them plan for the future, in case this situation comes up again.

A Wiz of a Solution

When I was teaching young children, I kept a wizard puppet in my classroom and let young children talk to the puppet when they were in conflict. I would have the puppet ask the questions and the students answer him. For some reason, the young students didn't get as upset or angry when they were directing their answers to the puppet instead of me.

Physical Conflict

One of the scariest things to deal with in the classroom is when your students become physically violent. When this happens, you become afraid that the two fighters will get hurt or hurt someone else. Usually, if they are small children, you can break them apart and deal with them. As they get older and bigger, it is not as easy. When this happens, you need to send for an administrator. Then you need to use your strongest, sternest teacher voice and tell them to stop. Never try to get between them or they could accidentally hurt you. Move all of the other students out of the room and into the hallway to keep them safe so they can't get hurt by flying fists or objects. Your main objective is to keep everyone as safe as possible. If possible, move all of the furniture away from the area where they are fighting.

Once administrators show up and help break up the fight and remove the fighting students, you need to get your students back into your room and settled down. You need to take a few calming breaths because at this point your adrenaline will be pumping through your body. Do not discuss the fight with your students, but listen if they are talking about it in case you get some insight into what may have caused the fight. Try to get your students back into your lesson to get their minds off the fight and back into learning.

You will need to write an office referral on both students involved in the fight. Each school will have a specific form and procedure for this event.

As soon as you can, write a statement about what happened. Write what was going on before the fight and what you were doing at the time.

Then write about your actions during the fight and after the fight. You might not need to do anything with this statement, but it is good to write about it while it is still fresh in your mind. An administrator will ask you to tell what happened, and then the consequences are dealt with by the administrator. Usually the students involved are sent home and suspended for a few days until further consequences are determined.

If the students return to class after being suspended, do not allow any students to discuss the fight, anything that caused it, or anything resulting from it. The students who were in a fight may even be a little anxious about your reaction when they return. It might be good to meet with each one privately to tell them that they will start the class with a clean slate. This may relieve some of the tension that everyone is feeling about their return.

DON'T TAKE IT PERSONALLY

The main things are for a teacher to remember are not to take bad behavior personally and not to judge a student just by their behaviors. I remember a time when I was frustrated with a fourteen-year-old student until I realized the circumstances that he was dealing with. He came to me with a chip on his shoulder and told me as soon as he met me that he was a lost cause. His last teacher had told him that he would be in jail before he turned eighteen. After I got over being shocked (which I think he wanted from me), I told him that he had a clean slate with me and we would work together to show that teacher she was wrong! I learned that his mom was a single parent and struggling with a drug addiction and his father was in jail for selling drugs, so my student was full of anger and a lack of self-esteem.

I used a lot of the strategies I've mentioned on improving his self-esteem. It took a long time and ample patience, but as he started experiencing success, he began to improve. At first there were only small things, but the more he succeeded, the more excited he became. He started to work harder and risked trying new things. If he didn't succeed, we talked about it and I had to keep reinforcing that an error was not a terror but instead an opportunity to improve. Soon his mistakes were not such a terrible thing and he was asking how he could fix the problem. By the end of the year he was smiling and proud of his achievements. Years later he contacted me to let me know that he is a pastor of a church and talks about me to others. This reminds me how important a teacher can be!

Understanding backgrounds shouldn't excuse behaviors, but it does help you understand why a student may be acting a certain way. You need to know what a student's home life is like and his relationship with his other family members. You may want to know if the student experienced some trauma or tragedy that contributed to his actions. I had a student who watched her mother get killed by the mother's boyfriend and was experiencing post-traumatic stress disorder. It took almost six months before I could get her to trust me and to even talk to me. Once I found out that she liked to draw, I was able to reach her on that level. She was able to express herself through art instead of through her behavior. This is a striking illustration of how once you know the student's background, you have a better shot at choosing the right strategies for dealing with and improving bad behavior.

Bullying

Actions that are repeatedly unwanted and aggressive toward others and involve misuse of power should be considered bullying.

If you see acts of bullying, they need to be addressed immediately. Bullying should not be tolerated at all. It should also be reported to the administration. Finding out why the aggressor is being a bully may help break the cycle of bullying. The bully may have low self-esteem and feel that bullying makes him look and feel tougher. If you can deal with the root of the problem, this student may realize that bullying is not an appropriate behavior.

As teachers, it is so easy to get caught up in this major anti-bullying movement and forget that we also need to teach students about natural peer relationships. Normal child development includes dealing with conflict—but it's important to know which situations merit the teacher's involvement.

Is It Bullying?

Not every negative peer action is bullying. It might just be a simple conflict that students need to learn how to deal with. Students may hurt one another's feelings or may be mean to one another, but this doesn't constitute bullying unless the child is repeatedly victimized.

Once you get both sides of the story, you need to see if all of the elements of bullying—power imbalance; unwanted, aggressive behavior; and repetition—are evident. If they aren't, then it was likely just a negative peer relationship and not an act of bullying. If the actions are considered bullying, then you need to refer the student to the administration, who will deal with it according to school policy.

When It's Not Bullying

We set our students up for failure when we allow non-bullying behaviors to be labeled as bullying. Students will feel like victims if you teach them that every negative peer relationship is bullying. In the workplace and in society, there will be negative peer relationships, and this is natural in any society. Many people in the workplace work in teams and have to learn how to deal with conflicts within the team. We can't eliminate this by treating everything as bullying.

You need to teach students coping skills and how to deal with negative peer relationships. Using role-play situations will help them prepare. Have students work in pairs for these activities or have two students act out the scenarios in front of the class. After the role-playing, discuss how each person acted and why. Also, discuss other ways the situation could be handled.

Some examples of situations and good student answers would be:

Situation 1: Your friend promises to do something with you and then other people invite him/her to do something with them at the same time. Your friend abandons you for the others.

- Tell your friend that you feel hurt and why you feel this way.
- Write this person a note about how you are feeling.
- Don't be accusatory, but share how this situation is making you feel.
- Find other friends to hang out with.

Situation 2: You walk up to a group of classmates who are talking about you. They are making fun of you.

- Walk away from this group and ignore them.
- Ask this group to stop talking about you and walk away.

Situation 3: You are working on a group project with three other classmates. One of your classmates calls your suggestion dumb. This hurts your feelings.

- Ask the others what they think about your idea.
- Insist that when you work as a team, no idea is dumb and everyone should be heard.
- Ask this classmate what other ideas she/he might have.

If the negative behavior continues, then this might become a different situation and could turn into bullying, but we should not treat every situation as if it is bullying from the start if it isn't necessary.

Parent Involvement

No parent wants to see their child hurt, and it is easy for parents to see any negative action toward their child as bullying. A parent wants to defend their child, and when a child complains about others, parents tend to rush to school and complain about bullying. They insist that actions be taken to punish this bully!

When this happens, you need to assure parents that you take this very seriously and that you will investigate the situation. Promise to let the parent know the result of your investigation. This is an important step in building trust and rapport with the parents. Following through with your promises is also vital.

If you determine that what's going on isn't bullying, you need to share this with the parents. Start off with sharing the definition of bullying. Then go through the behavior of the students and explain why this situation is the result of a negative peer relationship and not seen as bullying. Also explain that by mislabeling this situation, you could be causing more harm than good.

ENCOURAGING GOOD STUDENTS AND HELPING THEM FLOURISH

While you spend a lot of time working on the behavior plan and being consistent and fair with discipline, make sure that you don't overlook the good students. It seems that the students who act out can overshadow the ones who act appropriately. You want to make sure that the reverse happens in your classroom. You want the students who are good to shine and make the ones who misbehave want to do better. Remember to give the good students a lot of praise and recognition so that they don't copy negative behavior in order to get attention. When you call home to brag about the good behavior, the other students will ask why you haven't called their home. Let them know that you will call home and brag about them when they deserve it.

Get to know your students and the strengths they have. Many students are quieter and more modest about the things they are good at. Find ways to encourage them to use their strengths in their classwork. If they like to draw, have projects and assessments where they can use this to show their understanding of the material. If they have a dramatic flair, encourage them to dramatize important parts of the lesson for the class. If they like to sing, have them create a song or a rap to show their understanding of the material. If students like to make things with their hands, give them some clay and other arts-and-crafts supplies to make something to show their understanding of the material. Students may even have other suggestions of ways they can show their understanding, so encourage their input.

If you ask some students what their strengths are, some will tell you what they like to do. Some students may not even know that they have a talent or a strength, so keep your eye out for what they are doing and what they like to do. You may be able to help them discover a strength they didn't even know they had. When you give them a variety of activities to choose from, see which ones they tend to gravitate to and make sure you have those types of activities available for them in other lessons. Encourage them to explore and try different activities so they can find out which ones they really don't enjoy and which ones they enjoy more.

If you have students who participate in extracurricular activities, take time to watch them in this. If some students play a sport, go to a game and watch them. If your students play a musical instrument, go to a concert they are performing in. If your students are in a play, go watch a performance. Let them know the next day how much you enjoyed it. Taking time out of your own personal day will go a long way in encouraging them.

In this chapter, you learned about:

- Identifying bad behavior
- Handling students you don't like
- Building your students' self-esteem by giving them early successes and a motivating class motto
- Dealing with conflict, including student outbursts, verbal conflicts, and physical fights
- Dealing with your own emotions when you get upset
- Not taking bad behavior personally
- Identifying and dealing with bullying
- Spending more time encouraging good students than focusing on bad behavior

CHAPTER FIVE
Lesson Planning and Teaching

One of the reasons I became a teacher was my third- and fourth-grade teachers. After fifty years, I still remember their names.

In third grade, I had a teacher who made learning magical. She encouraged me and celebrated every learning victory I had. She helped me fall in love with learning! She helped me develop a love of reading. I was willing to try anything, risk anything, just so I could learn something new in her class. It was a safe place, and no one was ridiculed for making mistakes. It was a year that I excelled in learning, and I knew my family was so proud of me. I had dreamed of being a teacher from as early as I could remember, but she made me want to make my dream come true!

The next year, my new teacher got engaged, married, and divorced all in the one school year that I had her. Every day she screamed at us. She would rip students out of their chairs for making mistakes and even bang their heads against the wall. I was terrified. I was afraid to even ask to use the bathroom and sometimes wet my pants and I had the beginning of an ulcer. I was only in fourth grade. This teacher warned us if we went home and complained, she would kill us, so I guess no one ever told on her because this abuse continued all year long. I never told my family about this until after I graduated from college! I remember her wearing sunglasses in class and didn't realize until years later that she was being abused at home. I vowed that year that I was going to become a teacher no matter what it took and no student of mine would ever be afraid of making a mistake.

After having such an extreme experience, I wanted to be a teacher that students remembered for all the right reasons. I wanted students to feel that they would learn a lot in my classroom and were glad they had me as a teacher. I wanted to help students fall in love with learning as I had as a child, and if you're reading this book, I bet you do too!

In this chapter I'm going to talk about the importance of knowing the developmental stage of your students, knowing your students' learning styles, the importance of movement and relevance, and the general planning and teaching strategies that will make students fall in love with learning and create experiences that students will remember for their whole lives.

Teaching 101

At first it may seem like you are juggling a lot of balls, but once you get the hang of it, teaching will get easier. There are some things you need to remember to do all at the same time, but it just takes practice for all of it to come together. The things I mention here are the basics, and as you get more experience, you will be able to add more to your lessons. Just remember that it doesn't happen overnight, and the more you do these things, the more natural they will feel. Before you know it, you won't even have to think about doing these things. They'll become automatic.

Engagement

It is important to get and keep students engaged in learning. When they are challenged at the right level, they can be excited about learning. When they aren't bored or frustrated, they will take an active part in the learning process. If left bored and frustrated, they will find ways to disrupt the class and waste valuable instruction time. Knowing the students' developmental levels and learning styles will help to keep them engaged. Movement and relevance of the lessons are also important. Helping students work toward achievable goals can be tricky but is possible. Remember that even if students resist doing work, they really do want to succeed and might just be afraid of failure. Sometimes you may feel like a detective because you have to really work to find out what will motivate and engage your students, but once you figure it out, you can have high expectations of them. Usually, there's not one specific thing that will work for all of the students in the same way at the same time. Don't give up. Keep searching for the right key that will open the door to learning for your students. It may not be easy, but that's what it takes to have a great classroom.

Developmental Stages

Most teacher education programs teach Piaget's four stages of cognitive development. They are:

- Sensorimotor: birth through ages 18–24 months
- Preoperational: ages 18–24 months through age 7
- Concrete operational: ages 7 to 12
- Formal operational: ages 12 through adulthood

In the general-education classroom setting, you will usually deal with the concrete operational and formal operational stages. The age ranges given are usually accurate for the majority of general-education students, but there is no exact rule. Special-education students may be in the concrete operational stage longer than others or may never get out of this stage.

Knowing what stage the students are in developmentally is very important. Sometimes students have trouble learning the abstract skills because they haven't developed concrete foundational skills. If the students are in the concrete operational stage, you will need to use more manipulatives in the lesson to explain the concept you are trying to teach. When students are able to handle objects and move them around to understand a concept, they will remember it better. Once they understand it in this way, you can move to apply symbols to represent the concrete objects and help them move to more abstract thinking. Some may not be ready to move to the abstract thinking. If that's the case, it is all right to move back to manipulatives again.

I know that many schools and departments have a timeline that they want you to follow, but if you treat the timeline as more important than your students' mastery of the foundational skills, you are setting them up for failure. Many new teachers find this out the hard way. When students fail because they are rushed to meet timelines, they become discouraged, and soon they fall further and further behind. It is like using a chain that has several weak links. Would you want to use it to hold something together that might risk your life? No, because the weak links could break at a later time. This is what happens when we don't make sure that students have mastered foundational skills. Their weakness will break as they move to more complex skills, and it is harder to go back and fix all the weak links. It is worth taking the time to stop at the first sign of trouble and back up. Find the weak spot where the students need more help, then move forward from there.

Learning Styles

It is important to know if students are visual, auditory, or tactile-kinesthetic learners. Visual learners may prefer to see things in writing or have visual aids to help them complete their tasks. They may prefer to read stories and will comprehend better if they can see the words. Auditory learners do better when they hear directions or comprehend information better when it is told to them. Tactile-kinesthetic learners prefer to touch and/or move to help them learn. Students can have a combination of styles, depending on the situation, but they may prefer one style over others most of the time.

It is important that you teach to the students' learning styles and not your own learning style. Just because that is the way you learned best doesn't mean that is the way your students will learn best. Remember that you are teaching the students and not the lesson plans.

I am a very visual learner. I like to see what I am going to learn, look at examples, and get sequential instructions on paper. I remember being so excited about teaching this one lesson. I had lots of visuals. I had charts and posters to show my students. Rather than bore them by reading them, I told them they could use the visuals and follow the procedures listed. When I told them to begin their work, they seemed confused. While I ran around trying to help some students, others began talking and some started misbehaving. It was a disaster! Quickly I learned that this was not the way many of my students learned. Many of them were auditory learners and poor readers. Written instructions looked like a foreign language to them, and they could not complete the assignment without struggling. Yet when I read the instructions to them, they focused on what I was saying and then easily completed the assignment. Once they learned what the directions said, they could follow them more easily and use them as references.

It is important to look carefully at your goal for the lesson. If your goals are to teach them word decoding and reading comprehension, then you need to focus on the written word. This is the time to teach reading skills. But if you want them to learn content, giving them the information orally is okay. I noticed that when I read content information to students, they were engaged and excited about participating in the discussion. You could also let them listen to firsthand accounts of a historical event that was recorded and posted on the Internet. There are so many auditory options for students who learn this way. Once you have them invested in the lesson, then you can carefully insert reading material and help them as needed. You can learn through your discussions and activities whether they are understanding the material.

For tactile learners, having them write letters and words in sand or rice is very effective. Manipulating magnetic letters to spell words can help improve spelling and decoding skills. Using magnetic words in order to create new sentences will help students learn sentence structure. Drawing, painting, or even using clay may appeal to the student with this learning style.

When the school year begins, it is a good time to survey the students and discover what kind of learning styles they have. Ask for their input so that you can make learning more meaningful to them. Many are surprised that they have some input and are honest about how they prefer to learn. Explain to them that learning styles are like going into a grocery store. Every person will like and need different foods and no one's choices are better than someone else's choices. You should especially consider their learning styles when you give assessments. If you are interested in making sure they understand the content of a lesson, give them a few choices on how they can show you their understanding. This menu approach appeals to many students and gives them more power in their own learning. They may take a written test, give an oral report either to the class or record it for you to listen later, or they may draw a poster highlighting the important concepts they have learned. (I explain this in more detail in the section on Universal Design for Learning.)

LEARNING STYLES INVENTORY
Circle the numbers that describe you.

1. I like to learn by watching someone show me how. (V)
2. I like to learn by hearing someone tell me how. (A)
3. I like to learn by doing it while someone helps me learn how. (T/K)
4. I like to read books. (V)
5. I like to listen to recorded books. (A)
6. I like to read the directions as I do something. (V)
7. I like to have the directions told to me. (A)
8. I like to write stories. (T/K)
9. I like to tell stories. (A)
10. I like to act out stories. (K)
11. I like to dance. (K)
12. I like to sing. (A)
13. I don't like to sit still for a long time. (K)
14. I like teachers who write things on the board for me to follow. (V)
15. I like teachers who tell me what I need to do. (A)
16. I like to work when there isn't a lot of noise. (A)
17. Noise does not bother me. (V)
18. I can figure problems out if I can draw them out. (T/K)
19. I like to draw. (T/K)
20. I like to make things. (T/K)
21. I remember faces but not names. (V)
22. I remember names but not faces. (A)
23. I like to write reports instead of drawing. (V,T)
24. I like to draw posters instead of writing a report. (V,T)
25. I like to perform a skit instead of writing a report. (K)

Learning Styles:
V: visual, A: auditory, T: tactile, K: kinesthetic

Keep Them Moving

Students will learn better when movement is involved. I remember sitting for hours at my desk when I was a student, and when I got bored, my mind wandered. I remember watching others tap their pencils, bounce their legs, and swing their ankles. Not only is sitting for hours boring and tiring, but it is also really not good for anyone. There is so much talk about childhood obesity. Bringing movement into the classroom is one thing that a teacher can do to help combat this problem. When I had a student who fell asleep in class because he stayed up late playing video games, I had him stand beside his desk at the back of the room. This helped keep him awake, and he focused better. Now companies make furniture for students who need movement, such as wiggle chairs and stand-up desks. I always keep squishy balls or bendable sticks on hand for students who have to keep their hands moving.

Movement also helps students retain information. For instance, if you have students memorize the multiples of five from a piece of paper while sitting at their desks, it takes longer for them to remember the information. If you have the multiples of five written on the board or a screen and have students do jumping jacks while they recite the numbers, they will remember them faster and longer. Not only are students learning, but they are having fun too!

Dancing to grammar lessons can also be a lot of fun, and there are many videos online that students can watch and learn. Go Noodle (www.gonoodle.com) is a good website to go to if you want to see videos involving learning and movement. Sometimes when you want the students to show that they understand the material, you can let them create a song, a poem, or a dance to present to the class. Also, have them teach the song or the dance to the class, which involves lots of laughter and fun. This is so much better than just giving them a written test!

FIND OUT WHAT WORKS

One year I had a student who refused to do any assignment I gave him. It started as soon as he arrived and had to do the five-minute warm-up writing assignment. I had read his file and saw absolutely no reason why he couldn't do his work. I spent so much time disciplining him that it took up a lot of instructional time for the other students. I felt so frustrated and even angry because I wanted to teach and not be a disciplinarian! Some of the other students were feeling resentful, and the atmosphere in the class was not a good one. Even after meetings with his parents, who were extremely supportive, he wouldn't complete the assignments. I had tried taking away privileges in the classroom and the parents took away privileges at home, but that didn't work. We tried incentives to motivate him, but that didn't work either.

Finally, it hit me that I never asked my student what would work. I had a meeting with him and asked him what I could do to help him get his assignments done, and he requested to use the class computer. At the time we only had one computer in the classroom, which all of the students had to share, so it was a major reward to use the computer after all work was completed. I had never used the computer as an instructional tool but more as a motivational tool, so I decided to give it a try. For the first five minutes of class, I allowed him to do his writing on the computer because my goal was the content, not the handwriting. Amazingly, he completed the assignment. Eventually, I found out that holding a pencil was painful for him, and no one noticed during his previous nine years of schooling that he had a handwriting problem. I found programs that would let me scan worksheets into the computer and he could type up his answers. All of his tests were given this way also. He could use headphones and have the material read to him and then he could use the word processor for his writing. It was thrilling to watch his grades change from Fs upward to Cs, then Bs, and even some As. He was quite capable, but if I hadn't been willing to change the environment, we would never have known what he was able to do! Sometimes when nothing is working, it is time to step back and reevaluate and come up with a solution out of the box. I also learned an important lesson, and that was to include the student in the problem-solving discussion.

Brain Break

If you feel that students seem lethargic and not easy to motivate in the middle of a lesson, you might need to take a "brain break." Get the students out of the desk and have them jump in place. Have them do jumping jacks or put on some music and do a silly dance. This movement may be what they needed to get energized. After this short break, have them refocus on the lesson and you should see better results.

Make It Relevant

My husband was not a very good student when he attended school. He used to go in one door and then head out the back to go fishing. Many times, he told me that he felt it was all busy work and no one ever told him why he needed to learn this stuff. It wasn't until he was in the navy that the importance of learning was made clear to him. He learned that the information being taught was important for survival. He also learned practical skills that he would be able to use all his life, such as personal protection, navigational and medical skills. Once he realized that this information he was learning was not busy work and could be applied to real life, it had a different meaning. After that, he was motivated to learn and continues to do so even today.

When I first started teaching, my students would complain that a lesson was stupid, or they didn't understand the reason for learning that stuff. I started focusing on the reasons for teaching a lesson and sharing this reason with my students. Sometimes the skill they were learning was a foundation for future skills, and even though it might be boring, it might also be necessary. You should state the reason for the lesson on the board and make sure it is addressed during your introduction to the lesson.

I explain to older students that it is like learning to drive a car. No one can get behind the wheel of a car and start driving until they learn the basics. They have to study the manual and take a written test showing that they understand the rules of the road. No one goes for their first drive on the interstate. Instead they drive on smaller roads until they feel confident with their new skills. The same goes with learning foundational skills. We have to feel confident with them before moving on to more difficult or interesting skills.

As long as students can see that there is a reason for learning the material, they are more cooperative and open to new learning. When they aren't resisting, they are more engaged, are able to absorb more of the information, and are more able to apply their learning when needed.

Sometimes something happens in the news that takes precedence over a planned lesson. It is important to be flexible when this happens because this can be a great learning moment. When something is currently happening in the world, it makes learning more relevant and time sensitive. This happened to me when the space shuttle *Challenger* blew up and when the World Trade Center was bombed. When tragedies like these happen, it is better to address them than to ignore them. You might also be able to use current news in your lesson.

The Basics of Lesson Planning

The key to a great class is planning great lessons. We've talked about the overarching strategies and mentality that will set you up for success, so now it's time to get down to the actual art of creating engaging, relevant lessons that will ignite a love of learning and stick in students' minds for years to come.

You will need to plan two hours of activities for every hour of actual teaching. It is better to overplan than underplan because if students are bored, they will misbehave. Sometimes you will think a lesson will last longer than it actually does, so you should always include some extra activities just in case. You might not need them, but you will have them if you do.

You can even create a backup plan for extra activities that you can pull out anytime you have extra time in your classroom. These extra activities can review previous skills or units, so they don't involve new learning and students can work independently. For ideas on activities, see page 99.

Determining Students' Skill Levels

It is important to teach the student at the level they can learn. This takes some investigation and time.

If you are expecting to teach a class lesson on long division but a student is unable to even add or subtract, you are setting him up for failure. Yes, life would be much easier if all of the students were at the same exact learning point, but in reality, that never happens. Too many times, students fall through the cracks and never master the foundations before the teacher moves on to more difficult tasks. Rather than complaining about it, you just roll up your sleeves and get to work.

Planning and preparation before the actual teaching are vital to the success of any lesson! At the beginning of the school year, you should list all the lessons that you plan to teach in the sequential order that you need to teach them, along with an estimated time frame. These are usually called Long-Range Plans. After that, look at each individual lesson and write down the necessary skills the students must have in order to be successful with this lesson. Once you list the skills, make an assessment that the students can complete to show you that they are able to do these skills. You will then know the skills they can't do before they can move on to the lesson.

Assessment is very important to find out where the student's instructional level is. Using the preassessment, you can find out what skills the student already knows and which ones they don't. Don't waste time having the students sit through instructions they already know and understand just because others in the class don't understand them. I remember when I was in elementary school, I felt like the first month of every school year was spent on going over place value. I already knew and understood this concept and wanted to move on to more challenging skills, but I had to suffer through a month of boring instruction. I used to get in trouble for doodling or not paying attention because I was so bored. I have seen students have discipline problems because they are bored and not challenged.

Once students realize that they won't have to spend time doing work they already know, they become more engaged. They want to show what they are able to do when they take the preassessment. Tell them that this test won't be graded but will show you what skills they need to work on. Many students are skeptical at first until they understand this teaching strategy.

Working to an Individual Student's Skill Level

After the students complete the preassessment, make a checklist with all the necessary assignments needed to master the skill that they will be learning. Keep the checklist in a folder with that student's name on it. As they complete each assignment and you grade it, write the grade and the date on the checklist beside the assignment. After all the assignments are completed, give the post-assessment. Then record the score from the post-assessment and the date on the sheet as well. It helps students have a visual reference to what they are learning, so they can see their own progress, and it is a great reference to show at parent conferences too.

Students will work on their assignments while you walk around the room and give instruction to individual students when they need it. Since students are working on their own instructional level, you will be able to meet their specific needs. They can master the skills they need in order to move on to more complex skills. Students make more progress this way instead of working as a class on the same assignments.

Universal Design for Learning

Universal Design for Learning (UDL) is getting a lot of attention these days for good reason. Taking students' different learning styles into account and giving them a flexible learning situation is absolutely an effective and efficient teaching strategy. While it's a great technique, it's not really new. Over the years, I've heard it called individualized learning, differentiated learning, backward instruction, and personalized learning. When I was studying to be a teacher, it was just called "effective teaching" and we were taught to use different strategies to meet each student's needs. So in truth, successful teachers have been using UDL for many years even though they may not have always used that fancy name. The main thing to remember is that it works well when used in the classroom correctly.

UDL can be applied to every subject area on every level. Elementary school students to secondary school students all will benefit from UDL. This takes a lot of planning at first, but the more you plan your lessons this way, the more comfortable you will feel and the easier it will become. Soon it will become second nature.

Start by using the basic template for planning each lesson or unit, which is explained on the next page. It will be used in conjunction with your lesson plan. This will help you see the big picture. In the template, you'll fill in the learning style information for each student to see exactly what you need to plan for them in order to meet their needs. Some students may have more than one learning style, so you may want to use multiple methods to reach each student. As you continue planning new lessons, you will be able to refer back to previous plans to see what worked or didn't work for that student. Once you have the template filled out, you may see a way to group students who would benefit from doing the activity together. While you are tailoring the lessons to the individual needs of each student, you won't need to do thirty different activities or assessments for thirty students, as some will have overlapping learning styles and strengths.

The UDL Template

Use this template to chart students' learning styles and to tailor activities and assessments to their needs. For more blank templates you can copy and reuse in your classroom, see Appendix III.

Title of Lesson: Short Vowel Sounds

Goals and Objectives: Students will identify short vowel (SV) sounds

Student's Name:	*Learning Style	*Learning Style	*Learning Style	Assessment:	Activity 1	Activity 2	Activity 3
Cinderella	V A T K	V A T K	V A T K	Given 10 words, students will identify the words which contain SV sounds.	Shown flashcards with words, the student will pick the correct cards.	Given pictures of objects on cards. The student will pick out which ones have SV sounds.	Given a worksheet with words, the student will circle all words with SV sounds.
Peter Pan	V A T K	V A T K	V A T K	Given 10 words, students will identify the words which contain SV sounds.	When hearing words, the student will stop the reader when the word has a SV sound.	The student will listen to words on the flashcards and keep the flash card of the words that have a SV sound	Paired with another student, they will play a game reading words on flash cards. If it has a SV sound, they keep the card.
Snow White	V A T K	V A T K	V A T K	Given 10 words, students will identify the words which contain SV sounds.	Given alphabet magnets, students will form the words that have SV sounds.	Given a box with rice in it, the student will write the words that have SV sounds.	Paired with another student, they will play a game reading words on flash cards. If it has a SV sound, they keep the card.
Jiminy Cricket	K	V A T K	V A T K		When hearing words, the student will jump in place when he hears a SV word.	When hearing words, the student tosses a squishy ball from one hand to the other when he hears a SV word.	Given alphabet magnets, students will form the words that have SV sounds.

*Learning Styles Key: V (visual), A (auditory), T (tactile), K (kinesthetic)

Goals and Objectives: Think of the goal as the main reason students are learning the lesson and the objectives as the smaller steps to reach that goal. What do you want the students to know? Why is this important? If you can't determine the relevance, you need to rethink your goals and objectives. It is extremely important to always keep checking that what you want them to learn is relevant and not just busy work. Frequently stop and ask yourself why you want them to learn this and make sure that you are able to answer it.

Assessment: Next, how will you assess the mastery of this material? Your assessment may be different for individual students. Will this be an individual assignment or a group collaborative assignment? Creating rubrics is a great way to let students know ahead of time what criteria you will be using to measure their work. (See later in this chapter for more on rubrics.) Before they submit their final work, they can use the rubric to check that they have all the required components. After you grade the work, you can review the rubric with the student and explain how you determined their grade.

You need to create the assessment before you start teaching the lesson.

It is often better to have students create something rather than taking written tests. Many written tests have students regurgitate the information they are given but really don't show you that they know how to apply the information they learned. By creating something new, students are able to use their strengths to create something to demonstrate their knowledge (and as a bonus for you, they won't be able to cheat). Many students who don't test well will have a better chance of showing that they can master the skills you have taught.

Teaching: How will you teach the material? How will you manage the material that you want the student to learn? You need to take into account all of the students' learning styles. Are you reaching the students who are visual learners, auditory learners, and tactile-kinesthetic learners? There should be enough activities that involve all of these different learning styles.

What technology will you need? Are there specific devices or platforms that will work for some students to meet their needs? You may be able to record your directions so students who need to hear them again will be able to access them while allowing you to continue to work with other students. You may have digital photos of each step leading up to the final product. Visual learners will benefit from these. Some online programs will help students who need more practice with a skill or those who are visual and auditory learners.

Engagement: One way to help students retain their new information is by having them create projects. They can create posters, poems, movies, audio recordings, a dance, a sculpture, or any other creation they can think of as long as you approve it first. Once they have completed their creation, they need to present it to the whole class and explain what they have created and how it is relevant to what they have learned. Students learn by doing and will remember by sharing.

When students are engaged, your classroom may seem chaotic, but it is ordered chaos and the students are actively learning. This is very different from the passive learner where they are sitting and listening to the teacher talk. Each student is able to learn according to their own learning style and express themselves in a way that shows they understand the material and have mastered the skills that they have been taught.

By using Universal Design for Learning, your students will have a better chance of being successful in your classroom. Not only will they learn more, but they will also retain more of the information and be able to apply it when necessary.

Planning Activities

Once you know what you want your students to learn and that they can master it, you need to list the learning activities they can do. You want to make sure you have activities for students with all different learning styles. Let the students choose a certain number of activities, because giving students choices will help them stay engaged.

As you're planning the activities, ask yourself some questions: Do I want the students to work individually or in groups? Will I use learning centers? If at all possible, let students collaborate on projects because this is an important work skill. When students get in the workplace, they need to learn how to work with others, and those who have experiences collaborating in school are more successful when they enter the work force.

Once you know what activities you want the students to do, you need to develop the time frame. How long do I expect this lesson to last? Will it take one day, a few days, a week, or month? Having a tentative schedule will help everyone stay on track.

Gather Your Materials

Next you need to list all of the materials that you will need to have available for the students. If you need to get certain equipment, it is always smart to check with colleagues to see if they have any of the things that you might require. One time I was doing a science experiment even though I wasn't in the science department. Rather than buying expensive science equipment for this one lesson, I checked with the science department chair, who let me borrow some of the equipment. I made sure they were clean and in good shape when I returned them.

Are there any things that the students will need to supply? Having this information will save a lot of time and confusion once the students start working. Letting students know beforehand also helps them come prepared. Some students could split the cost of things that are bought in sets rather than single items. This preparation decreases the chances of students sitting around being bored because they don't have the right materials.

Project Presentation

The last important step is how you plan for the students to share their information. Sharing their projects helps students retain the information they have learned. If this step is missed, the project and the new information will easily be forgotten. I can still remember some of the projects that I learned in elementary school because I remember having to present the project to the class. I'm sure that I did projects in other classes, but why don't I remember them? Probably because I just submitted them but never shared them with others.

Teaching Your Lessons

How you teach your lesson can impact how well students stay engaged and retain information. Every lesson should begin with an introduction and then an explanation of your assessment before you get into the meat of the lesson. After that, your procedures need to be organized in a way that will make sense to your students.

Introducing a Lesson

It is important to find something that grips students' attention and makes them want to learn more. This might be a video clip, a demonstration, or reading an excerpt or poem. You need to know the personalities of your students and what might be best suited for them. If it is the beginning of the year, it is usually safe to start with a video clip. You want to make sure that you are enthusiastic and excited about teaching your lesson. Enthusiasm can be contagious and you want your students to be excited about learning something new. You want them to see the possibilities and opportunities that this new lesson will bring them. This introduction can make or break a lesson right from the start.

At this time, you should give them some background information about the topic and share with them why you think this is important for them to learn.

Procedures

After the introduction, you want your students to understand the assessment at the end of the lesson. They need to know what you expect them to get from the lesson before they start on their activities. I know that when

I have taken classes, I was distracted from learning the new information because I kept wondering how I would be tested on the information. A thorough explanation takes the mystery out of the assessment so the students can focus on the learning. If you are going to use any rubrics, this is the time to show and explain how they will be used. It would be good to give the students a copy of the rubric you will use, so they have a reference to follow as they are working. This is also the time to give the deadline for completing the work.

Next, explain the activities that you will want them to do. There might be a certain activity that you want everyone to complete, but let them choose a certain number of other activities that you've designed to fit different students' learning styles, skills, and needs. Make sure you explain all of the activities before allowing students to begin working. You might prefer to create a worksheet with the activities listed, circle the ones you require them to complete, then let them circle the ones they want to complete. This visual helps them stay on track.

If a project is going to take multiple days, it is important to spend the last five or ten minutes of each class checking with each student and seeing what work was accomplished. This keeps them accountable for staying on task and completing their work.

At the beginning of the class after the first day, it is good to take five minutes to ask students if they are having any problems or if they have learned anything exciting that they want to share with the class. This sharing helps to keep the enthusiasm level up and it lessens the disruption during class when students want to share while others are working.

Plan at least one or two days (depending on the number of students you have) for students to share their finished projects.

Presentation of Material

At first you may choose to teach directly out of textbooks. Many textbook publishers give teacher guides with suggestions for how to teach that chapter. As you get more comfortable teaching the topics, you may want to pull material from several sources and create your own content that you want the students to use. This helps keep the students from being overwhelmed or distracted with information that you don't plan on teaching them. Some textbooks may not give all of the information you want the students to have or explain things at the level of detail you would like.

After the introduction, you can work with the whole class on the new material. Students may read aloud the textbook information or the teacher-made material. To check for understanding, you will have a question-and-answer time or a discussion about the material that you have read together. You may even have videos or visual aids to present to the class.

After the whole-group portion of the lesson is complete, students will begin the activities that you explained earlier. They may be working individually or in small groups.

Tips on Adjusting Lesson Plans That Aren't Working

Sometimes the lesson you are teaching is not working. The students don't seem to pay attention and are bored. Their reactions are influencing your actions and you get flustered and frustrated. When this happens, it is time to take a deep breath and regroup. You have several options.

Don't be afraid to postpone a lesson that's falling flat. Tell the students that they seem to be having trouble focusing and you are going to postpone this lesson for another time. Don't tell students that their lack of focus means you are scrapping the lesson, because this can become a learned behavior to avoid doing lessons they don't like.

This is when you can break out one of your backup activities. It can be a good time to do something that involves movement and music to energize the students. After this energizing activity, they may be ready to return to the lesson. You might also give them an activity on the same topic first and then give them this lesson after that.

If you postpone this lesson for another day, you may need to reflect on why the lesson isn't working. Be honest with the students and say that you notice the lesson isn't working. The lesson has important concepts or skills that they need to learn so ask for their input on how to make it work better for them. Some students may need more visuals to understand the lesson or some students may not understand the relevance of the lesson. Students are surprised that you asked for their input, and they tend to be more engaged in the lesson when you implement their suggestions.

You might have to totally scrap the lesson you have planned and redo it. Talk with colleagues and explain you are struggling with teaching a concept or skill and your lesson just wasn't working. Other colleagues may have helpful suggestions because they have a different perspective.

Sometimes I actually talk about a lesson with family or colleagues before I teach the lesson and mention some of the activities. Luckily, I've had someone tell me that they didn't think it would work and gave me reasons. I was able to tweak my plan before I taught it and it turned out to be a better lesson than it would have been before I changed it.

Don't feel like a failure if a lesson doesn't work. Sometimes teaching is a trial-and-error process and what worked with one group of students at a different time might not work with the current group of students. All students are different with different needs, and it is impossible to know exactly what each student will need when planning a lesson. It is important though to figure out how to fix the lesson so it can work.

Grading and Testing

Implementing effective grading rubrics and assessments that really tell you if students are grasping the material is foundational to a good classroom. These practices let you know if your strategies are working, who needs more help, and who's shining. Grades and tests are not necessarily the ends themselves, but instead they can be the means by which you can see not just how the students are doing, but how you're doing as well. The assignment you are assessing will determine the kind of assessment you should use. You should base your assessment on the goals that you planned before you start teaching the material. No matter what assessment you use, your system for testing and grading needs to be clear and fair. And, of course, you have to take standardized testing into consideration.

Rubrics for Grading

A rubric is a scoring tool in the form of a chart that a teacher can use to evaluate student work. It gives specific criteria to use and a numeric scale for each one. This helps the teacher evaluate each student's work by the same measures. When complete, the score for each criterion will be added together to give a final evaluation score. Rubrics are great tools for students to use before turning in their work as well as for teachers when they're grading. You can determine the specific criteria that you want in an assignment and figure out the student's grade from this. Once the criteria are determined, you need to come up with a rating scale for each criterion. Simple rubrics are easier to understand and follow, so I recommend using a 0–3-point scale. Some rubrics may use a 0–5-point scale, but I think anything over 5 points is too confusing to use effectively. You can search online for premade rubrics, and there are even some sites that will help you develop a rubric to print out. Some teachers just use a spreadsheet to design their rubrics.

Writing: If the student gets the rubric before writing, they can use it to help them proofread their work before turning it in. This will also allow them to make sure they do everything that is needed when writing. You can determine the number of sentences that should be written, the number of paragraphs, specific punctuation you want used, sentence structure, and content information. Then you need to determine the rating scale you want. For example, the rating scale might show the following criteria: Sentences—0 points for less than five sentences, 1 point for a minimum of five sentences, 2 points for six to ten sentences, and 3 points for anything over ten sentences. Punctuation ratings may include 0 points for no use of punctuation, 1 point for no more than two errors, 2 points for one error, and 3 points for no errors.

Individual Projects: If you have students create a new project from their learning, there is no danger of cheating and you can allow students to express their knowledge in ways that they are comfortable with. After reading a novel, for example, I had a student create a sculpture in his welding class and it was fabulous! Students can create posters, clay sculptures, perform skits, or write a song. You can allow them the freedom to determine the type of project as long as they meet your basic criteria. A rubric helps you stay consistent and fair when grading projects and it makes grading much easier. Again, the student will have the rubric before beginning the project and will know if the project is going in the right direction. A sample rubric might include criteria for creativity, neatness, presentation, amount of information given, proper spelling/punctuation, and accuracy of information.

Math Tests

For math skills, you can give a preassessment of specific math skills to see exactly what area the student is weak in and what skills need to be taught. This is given at the beginning of the year with a sample of all the skills that you want to teach during that year. Then you would give a preassessment before each specific unit so you know what skills need to be taught. After you teach the skills and allow the students time to practice, a post-assessment with similar questions as the preassessment will show you whether the student has mastered that skill and is ready to move on.

Group projects: Students working in a group can also check their project according to a rubric and see what else may need to be done in order to improve their grade. The same rubric that you use for individual projects can be used for group projects. Be careful when assessing group work so that one person isn't doing all of the work and the others getting the credit. Ask students to break up the project into separate duties and submit with the project what each person did. You can also include in the rubric a section that includes an individual component.

Evaluating the Merit of the Assignment Itself: Your rubric will evaluate the teaching effectiveness of the project itself. This will help you analyze what changes you can make when assigning future projects. Your rubric can include student engagement, student understanding, student independence, available materials, resource materials available, and overall satisfaction with the final projects.

Traditional Tests: Traditional tests are usually given after teaching a specific topic or unit. They include multiple choice, true/false, short answer, and essay questions. A simple answer key can be used to grade these tests (instead of a rubric). Depending on the student, some questions may work better for them than others. The multiple choice, true/false, and short answer questions require the students to memorize answers more than applying them. An essay question is more suited for having students restate the information but also allows them to give reasons for their answers. These kinds of assessments may tempt some students to cheat, so teachers have to keep a watchful eye when administering the test.

Standardized Testing
All teachers are involved with standardized testing procedures in some way. You may have to administer the test, or you may have to monitor the test. Both roles are equally important. And, of course, you will have to help your students prepare for their tests.

Administering/Monitoring Standardized Test
There will be a general meeting where you will be instructed of your duties and given a booklet with written directions. Read these very carefully and make sure you understand the exact procedures that you need to follow. On the day of the test, you also will have to sign a form promising that you won't break confidentiality laws and help students cheat on the test. Follow directions to the letter. There will be rules about taking charts and formulas off the walls before the

tests are administered. Check to see if your students need to have any accommodations for standardized testing. Usually, a special-education teacher or guidance counselor will know which students need accommodations. Once you find out who needs accommodations, make sure these are available before the test is given and that the student receives them on test day.

Preparing for Standardized Tests

You won't be able to know the exact questions on a standardized test, so you shouldn't try to "teach for the test," but there are still things you can do to prepare for the test. Good preparation will help the students get higher scores, and there are ways you can work important standardized testing topics and skills into your normal lessons throughout the year. This will help prepare students without constantly drilling them about testing. Standardized tests can be an important but exhausting event for the whole school. Encourage students to take it seriously but remind them that that no matter what happens, it is not the end of the world.

Right Before the Test

Encourage your students to get a good night's sleep and eat a good breakfast. Let the parents know when the standardized test is scheduled to be given. Make sure they know what materials to bring to the test and have extra writing utensils available on the day of the test. When students arrive, greet them with a smile and try to put them at ease.

Vocabulary

Throughout the year, you can also teach students the important vocabulary that they might see on the test. There may be content-specific vocabulary that students are expected to know for each grade. Knowing specific vocabulary will help students understand the questions better in order to come up with the right answer. Your department head should be able to direct you to where you will find this information for your grade and content area.

Math Skills

For math, you need to teach solving math word problems, as many standardized tests focus on these. Some students struggle with this important life skill and need lots of practice throughout the year. Many students struggle with determining the correct operation to use when solving word problems. There are key words to look for in every word problem that will give students clues to which operation is needed. It might be good to have a chart showing the key words to look for and the operation called for. Seeing a visual often helps students retain this information for the test.

Writing Skills

Give students lots of opportunities to practice writing skills. The more they do this, the easier it will be for them. Writing often will help them feel more comfortable when they have to produce writing on demand. Have students look for grammatical and spelling errors so they can practice proofreading skills. They will need to proofread their work before submitting it on the test.

All of the practice you do with the students will help them prepare for the test without "teaching to the test." They should be able to apply the skills that you taught them to the questions they are given and feel more confident when taking the test.

After the Test

Many students are exhausted and stressed out after a standardized test is given. Be aware that they may act out or be moody and need time to relax. This is a good time to have some recreational reading, listen to music, or even go outside to get rid of excess energy. Different students have different needs, so it is important to keep things calm and give students time to regroup and reenergize. Remember that you shouldn't talk about specific questions given on the test.

In this chapter, you learned about:
- Teaching to different developmental stages
- Working with different learning styles
- Motivating students through movement
- Making lessons feel relevant to students' lives
- Discovering and following students' dreams
- Overcoming students' resistance to lessons or assignments
- Using your failures as opportunities to do better
- Setting high expectations so students can do their best
- Planning lessons based on students' skill levels and learning styles using Universal Design for Learning
- Setting lesson objectives, assessments, and getting student engagement
- Planning activities
- Introducing and carrying out lessons
- Adjusting lesson plans that aren't working
- Creating rubrics for assessments and projects
- Preparing for standardized testing without "teaching to the test"

Activity Suggestions

Here are some activity suggestions that you can use in the classroom. They can be adapted for your students' age and educational level.

Read Aloud

Reading aloud to students is a great activity to start your class. Some students have never had a book read aloud to them, so this may be a new experience for them. This can be done with students of all ages because it encourages them to read and it improves their listening skills.

At first they may have trouble sitting still and listening. Start off with a few pages. After reading, ask students some questions about what you read. Ask them to name the main characters and describe them. Ask someone to summarize what you read. Have them predict what will happen next. When you start reading the next time, review the main characters and have someone say what has happened up until this point. This is great for those who have forgotten or were absent.

Pick a book that you think students will find exciting and interesting. Then read for about five to ten minutes at the beginning of class. You might do this every other day. Students will start begging you to read on the days it isn't scheduled because they want to find out what will happen. I have read books such as *The Phantom Tollbooth, Harry Potter and the Sorcerer's Stone, My Teacher Is an Alien,* and *From the Mixed-Up Files of Mrs. Basil E. Frankweiler.* I have read these books to everyone from high school students down to elementary school. Sometimes it encourages students to ask questions and do research on topics that might have been mentioned in the books. Plan on reading aloud at the beginning of class because this gives students time to settle down and prepare to do classwork.

Field Trips

Going on a field trip is a wonderful enrichment activity for your students!

Depending on the age and the grade of the students, there are many interesting places to take them. The usual field trips that school groups go on are to local museums, zoos, and state capitols. Younger children enjoy a trip to the grocery store and public library. Checking with your local tourism bureau will also give you some great ideas. I found out that we have a granite quarry in our area, and when I called them, they were willing to give my high school students a tour. They also talked about job opportunities available to students when they graduate. Check with different manufacturing plants in your local area because many will give school groups a tour. Some car manufacturing plants give tours. Not only will they learn how a car is assembled, but they will be able to see different jobs that are involved in the process. Visiting a local bank will help students learn about finances. If you have public transportation in your city, you can contact their main office and see if you can have someone teach your students how to plan and ride the bus or train system. This may involve actually going through the process of riding on the bus or train as a class.

First, make sure you know the school and district requirements before planning the trip. It is always important to get administrative approval before letting your students know about the trip. If you don't have permission, you don't want to disappoint the students.

Once you get permission, work out a timeline to determine how much time is needed to schedule transportation, permission slips, and other details. Find out the cost of the transportation and any other fees that may be included for your entire class, including yourself. Then divide the cost of the trip by the number of students who will be going. You may also need to touch base with the bookkeeper to discuss how you take money for the trip and write receipts for the money.

Send home permission slips as soon as you get the trip set up, so you will have time to collect the money and the slips before the field trip. Make plenty of copies of the permission slip because students will lose them and need another one. No one should be allowed to go on the field trip without a permission slip and an emergency contact number given. Write a receipt for the money as soon as you get it. Do not ever hold money in an unlocked location where it might disappear! Any lost money is your responsibility, so turn it in to the bookkeeper as soon as possible.

Have a deadline for the return of permission slips because sometimes you need a specific number of students in order to go on the trip and to pay for the cost of transportation. A week before you go on the trip, contact the transportation company and confirm the date and time they will arrive to pick up your class and when they will pick you up to bring you back to school. Also, call the destination to confirm that they know you are coming. There have been trips scheduled when the bus company had the wrong date written down but the teacher was able to correct this before the day of the trip. It would be a disaster to have the students ready to leave for a trip but no bus arrives!

If you have to leave students behind, make sure you know who will be supervising them while you are away from school. You will also need to have assignments prepared for them to do while they are at school.

If any students need medication during the trip, make sure you have the appropriate permissions and don't forget to bring the medicine on the trip. Make sure you don't forget to give the student their medicine at the appropriate time.

Know what procedures you need to follow in case an emergency happens. Have the school phone number handy because, during an emergency, you may forget the number.

Make sure you talk about behavior expectations before going on the trip. Also, make sure you have the required number of chaperones for the trip. I like to break my class into groups along with one adult chaperone.

I give the chaperone a list of the students in the group and ask them to make sure they know where these students are at all times.

Count the number of students when they get on and off the bus each time. During the trip, check with the chaperones on a regular basis to make sure they know where their students are and that there are no problems. Nothing is worse than telling a parent that you left their child behind on a field trip!

When you get off the bus at your destination, make sure you check with the bus driver for the time and location you will be picked up to return to school. Are students allowed to leave things on the bus, and will it be locked if the bus driver leaves it? Will students need to take their lunch with them, or will you be returning to the bus to get lunches?

When you return to class the next day, have students reflect on the field trip. Have them share something that they learned. What was the best part? Students can draw about their trip. Others may record a reflection or write about it, and their work can be shared with the whole class. Sometimes when one student shares a memory, others will chime in with more details or add their memory of the same event. This really energizes students.

Reflect on your trip and your planning. How did the trip go? What went well? What did not go as planned? What would you do differently on your next trip? Keep these notes for future field-trip planning.

Jeopardy!

Let's face it, reviewing work for a test can be boring. Try to make reviewing fun for students. I know that people say we shouldn't have to entertain students, but in today's world, it makes life a lot easier. Most people would rather study in an entertaining way than be bored to tears.

Make games that you can play as a class and that can be used at a later time individually for review. You also want it to be self-checking as much as possible. It doesn't do any good for them to study the wrong answers. This only leads to wrong learning and frustration. It also takes up a lot of time if you have to stop what you are doing to go check their answers, and it defeats the purpose of teaching students how to study independently.

One game that has been a hit for years is *Jeopardy!* This game has been long-lasting on television, so I know most of the students have seen it. Even if they don't know the game, it is easy to learn. My version of the game isn't exactly like the television version, but it is close. This game is great for midterms and final exams.

I know there are digital templates out there to make this game for computer use, but I'm always afraid that technology might not be working the day we play the game or I might not have access to a screen that all of my students can see, so I like to make my own using poster board, plain envelopes, and index cards.

It takes some time to make, but once it is made, it can be used over and over again. I make the game on poster board with pockets for the number of columns for each category and the number of rows for each dollar amount. I cut a long envelope in half and then glue the half envelopes as pockets for each spot. I try to have five to seven categories. I also have five rows for the dollar amounts and another row for my category names. In each pocket, I will put in an index card with a question on the front and the answer written small on the back corner. Then I cover it with another index card showing a dollar amount, increasing in hundred-dollar increments.

I take the material that I want them to know and put them in separate categories. These categories are put in the top pocket of each column. I write down one question on each index card with the answer written on the back in a corner. On the back, I also write down which category the question belongs in, so it is easier to set the game up later. This is great because students can use these cards to review independently when we aren't playing the game. I rotate the questions in the pockets when we repeat the game after someone wins.

Students take turns and request a category and dollar amount. I read aloud the question and the student answers it. (I don't require my students to give their answers in question format.) If they answer correctly, they keep the dollar amount card. If they answer incorrectly, I let the next student answer the question and continue asking students until the question is answered correctly. Whoever answers it correctly keeps the dollar amount card and then the next student has a turn. This continues until all of the questions have been answered. Students add up their dollar amount cards and the one with the most money wins the game.

If we repeat the game, I let a student reset the dollar amounts while I put the questions I used to the side and put new questions up if I have more cards that haven't been used.

When I'm creating a written exam, I will have all my questions already prepared and just transfer them into test form. So, even though this may take time to create at the beginning, it does save time later on.

I am always surprised how engaged the students are when we play this game. They get competitive and are so proud when they get the answer right. I'm also pleased with how this helps students remember a lot of the material I want them to know. When students finish their individual work, they are willing to study the cards so that when we play the game, they have a better chance of winning. I have never had a class that didn't enjoy this game for review.

Song Lyrics
Using song lyrics of current popular songs is a great tool, because they help students practice reading skills such as decoding and comprehension. You also have control over the content and the language, while students get a kick out of working with something that is current and relevant to their lives.

Song lyrics can also be used to discuss what message the songwriter is trying to send. If there is a rhyming pattern in the stanzas, it would make a great poetry lesson. If there are historical or science references, these can be further investigated. Any locations mentioned can be used for a geography lesson.

Song lyrics are great to introduce poetry. Usually, students don't understand why we study poetry. It is shocking to them that song lyrics can be considered poetry. It may also teach students another way to express their feelings.

You can try to find an older song from a different generation that is sending the same message. Let students compare the two songs. How does the language differ? Why was this older song popular back then? What is the message both songwriters are trying to convey?

Get Outdoors

Get students outdoors as much as possible. Fall and spring are wonderful times to get students outdoors. We often hear how much time students spend behind computer screens, so this is a great opportunity to get them away from screens. Being outdoors involves movement and keeps students active. Being outdoors works for any subject area and any age group but especially elementary school age. Don't be afraid to change your setting as long as you get administrative approval. Make sure you have your behavior plan established also. If you are doing a writing lesson about leaves, or even changes that are happening, get outside and let them write. Have them observe the world around them! If they have a math lesson, figure out ways to incorporate the outdoors into your lessons. Not only is this fun, but it makes the lesson more relevant to students. They will become more engaged and remember better. Being outdoors can encourage exciting science discussions as students discover new things about nature. The world outside is an exciting place if we allow students to explore the possibilities.

Outdoors Journal: Have students keep an Outdoors Journal. Encourage them to use their senses (except taste!) and write down their observations. What do they see, hear, smell, and feel? These observations can be used in a later writing assignment. Have them draw some of the things they see. At first this may seem difficult for students because they are not used to doing this. The more they do it, the better they will get at observing things and hearing things. You should take your students out for fifteen minutes once a week to write in their journals. After a few weeks, they will start to notice more and then notice changes that are occurring. When they start observing nature, they will be curious about what they are actually seeing and learn to identify some common trees and plants. They will be listening to different sounds, and soon their curiosity will make them want to identify birds that you are hearing.

This leads to further investigation and research. Sometimes curiosity is the best teacher.

After you return to the classroom, ask students if they want to share anything special from their journals. The quiet students may have lovely sketches, and sometimes another student will ask them to share their drawings. This is a great way to encourage the quiet students to share and spend time in the spotlight.

Leaf Rubbings: Students of all ages really enjoy making leaf rubbings. Have students find different types of leaves with lots of texture. Have them put the leaf on a hard surface with the textures facing up. Put a piece of white paper over it and use a pencil or crayon to rub over it. Students can make separate leaf rubbings or a collage of leaves all on one white piece of paper. After making the rubbings, have students use resources such as tree identification books or the Internet to identify what kind of tree the leaf came from.

Listening to Nature: Have students sit outside quietly for ten minutes. Record this on your phone or a recorder if possible. Have students make a list of everything they hear. If you need to, you can always relisten to the recording to refer to different sounds that were heard that the other students missed. Doing this every other week or at least once a month can help improve listening skills.

Creative Writing: Have students sit outside and look around them. Have them pretend they are something in nature and write a story about their day from that point of view. Students might pretend to be a tree, a leaf, a bird, a squirrel, or even an acorn.

Learning New Vocabulary: Have students find evidence of specific vocabulary you are learning. Some examples of vocabulary could be chlorophyll, metamorphosis, larvae, nymph, mammals, insects, spiders, or flower parts.

Weather Record: Students create a daily record of the weather, including the temperature. They can make a chart showing the changes in the temperature over time.

Nature Bingo: Prepare a bingo board (you can determine how many squares according to the students' ages) with different items in nature to look for. Have students find each item and take a photo with a phone or iPad for evidence. If they find all of the things on their board, they return to you with all the evidence. Every student who finds all of them can win a prize like a pencil or a sticker.

Rock Art: Students may enjoy painting rocks and then, using a Magic Marker, writing a motivational message. Afterward, take them outside and encourage them to hide the rocks so that others will get a pleasant surprise when they find them. This encourages creativity, and by writing a motivational message, they are also encouraging themselves.

Bird Feeders: One favorite activity for any age in the winter is to coat a pinecone with peanut butter and then roll it in birdseed. Hang these from trees near your classroom window. Students can watch the birds eat the seeds from inside the classroom. Encourage students to try to identify the birds.

Exploring the Square: Give each student the same length of string/yarn to make a big square on the ground. Students find a place outside where they want to make their square. Then have students make a list of everything they see in that square. Encourage them to get close to the ground to see the small things. Give them a magnifying glass to see the smaller things. If you have a camera, write their name on a slip of paper and put it above their square, then let them take a photo of their square to look at later.

CHAPTER SIX
Co-teaching

Co-teaching is when two teachers who are equally qualified to teach join forces and teach a group of students in one classroom. Each teacher will have different strengths to bring to the table. Students will benefit from having both teachers because they get more attention and will be more effectively taught. This is different than a classroom having a teacher's aide where there is only one certified teacher and the other person is support personnel for the teacher. Co-teaching can be an effective way of teaching if it is done correctly. In order for this to occur, it will take a lot of planning and communication between both teachers and full support of the administration.

The hardest thing about co-teaching is putting egos aside to get on equal footing. One teacher is not better than another, but instead, both have different strengths to bring to the table. I have taught with another teacher who thought I knew nothing because she was the content teacher. It was a struggle to work with her because I felt I was constantly proving myself. While I might not have had the in-depth knowledge about the content, I had in-depth knowledge of different strategies that could help a student succeed. I have also taught with a teacher who felt like I was the expert and she wasn't. Of course, this made me feel like I was doing all of the work and she backed off and acted like a teacher's aide instead of a co-teacher. It is important that both teachers speak up and understand that each has individual strengths.

A Good Start

To get off on the right foot, it is important to have an initial meeting with the administration in which you and your co-teacher meet and talk about your ideas for the classroom. It is important for both teachers to feel that the administration is backing them both and that both have equal footing in the classroom. Both teachers need to learn to trust each other and agree if there are any problems, they will talk it out with each other before going to an administrator. This partnership is like a marriage, and without communication, the partnership will not work.

Make a Plan

Communication is key! Planning the big picture and developing a long-range plan together is important. This helps both teachers know the time frame that they are working with to get through specific lessons. Once this is established, weekly and/or daily plans can be tentatively scheduled. These plans should include the objective of the lesson and how this objective is going to be assessed.

When talking about instructional strategies, it needs to be decided who will be responsible for which activities. During a particular lesson, one teacher always needs to take the lead role. Having two leaders at any one time will only confuse students. One teacher may be more confident in teaching the content of a particular lesson and another is more confident in helping struggling students. The next time a new lesson is taught, these roles may be reversed. One teacher might enjoy teaching a specific topic or the other teacher might be excited about teaching a specific activity.

Both teachers need to plan a time every day to communicate about the day and expectations. In the beginning these meetings may take longer, and as the year progresses, long meetings will no longer be needed. These planning times are the opportunity to work all the particulars out so that when the students arrive for the lesson, everything can run smoothly. The confidence of the two teachers working together will help the students feel more comfortable with learning new concepts. I know that some teachers actually schedule a regular time to plan together each day. Sticking to this schedule keeps things from falling through the cracks. It is also important to decide who is in charge of getting the materials together, how the assessment of the material will work, and even who will be grading the work. If the planning is done in detail, things should run smoothly.

Here is a sample plan for a class:
Gathering materials—Teacher B
Introduction to the lesson—Teacher A
Content lesson—Teacher B
Explanation of assignment—Teacher A

Teacher A takes a small group who may need more individual help to a separate area of the room.

Teacher B helps the rest of the class.

Summary of the lesson—Teacher B
Grading of assignment—Teacher B
Recording grades—Teacher A

On another day for another lesson roles may be reversed. If a test is given, one teacher may take a small group who needs accommodations for testing to a separate area or even another classroom. The other teacher will stay with the larger group.

Fun Activities

There are many fun activities that can be done in a classroom when there are two teachers. When learning history or reading a novel, some students may choose to do a dramatization and video record it. This recording may need to be done in a different location, so having an extra teacher to supervise this is handy. Another activity may involve a scavenger hunt around the school looking for clues or measuring different items around the school as a math lesson. Again, the second teacher can supervise the hunt. There may be science experiments that can be done in separate learning centers but need an adult there for safety reasons.

Reflection

Another important thing to do during co-teaching is the reflection. After each lesson or major unit, it is important for both teachers to reflect on how it went. This is where they can discuss what worked and what didn't. Once they establish these things, they can decide what they did right and what they need to change for the next lesson. I think without this reflective piece, it is hard for both teachers to grow in this co-teaching situation. If things aren't working, they will just continue to not work, and both teachers will feel a lot of dissatisfaction in their positions.

Resolving Conflicts Together

During the initial meeting with your co-teacher, it is good to discuss in advance how you will resolve any conflicts. By planning lessons and duties ahead of time, you should be able to resolve any conflicts with teaching strategies. The more you communicate and learn each other's styles, the easier it will be to plan using each other's strengths. If you disagree, try to compromise. Offer to do it one way this time and then do it the other way next time. If you still feel you can't resolve your conflict between yourselves, it is time to bring in an administrator.

....

In this chapter, you learned about:
- Starting off on the right foot
- Making a plan together
- Reflecting with your co-teacher on how your teaching is going
- Planning activities to do with a co-teacher
- Resolving conflicts you may have with a co-teacher

....

CHAPTER SEVEN

Teaching Students with Disabilities

Even though some students may be identified as having a specific disability, these labels don't define them. Just because a number of students may have the same label does not mean that they can all be taught in the same way. Some strategies that typically work for a certain disability may not work for all the students with that disability. It is important to have strategies for different disabilities, but it is just as important to teach to the individual student and not the label attached to their disability. While we will go through some specific disabilities in this chapter, we will talk about a variety of ways to teach students of all abilities.

Autism

Whether you teach general-education students or special-education students, you may have a student with autism in your class. It may seem daunting at first, but if you look at it like a different learning style, then a world of possibilities opens up to you. Some of the suggestions I give that work well with students who have autism may also help some students who don't have autism. There is no magic solution for this broad diagnosis, but there are a number of strategies you can use to create a great learning environment for these students.

Visual Schedules

Depending on the age of the student, these schedules may vary. Pictures may be used with the nonreader, and words alone may work for the higher-level reader. Giving a schedule helps the student prepare for what is expected. A student with autism sometimes does not like surprises and changes in routines. Having a visual schedule helps him process any changes that may occur and also helps the transition from one activity to the next. Post a schedule on your board to keep students on track with the activities that you want them to accomplish. Give advance warnings of a transition that will take place. You could use a visual timer to prepare them for a change. Let them know that in two minutes they will be expected to do something different. Then, when it is time to change, the move won't be as upsetting for them.

Choices

Whenever possible, give students choices of which task they want to complete first. Give the students two or three options but no more than that. They can do one first and then the others, but let them know that all of the tasks must be completed. Usually, students feel powerless in school, so having choices helps them feel like they can control something in their lives.

Task Analysis

All students can benefit from this. Make a list of the exact process that the student needs to follow in sequential order to complete a task. This also helps with planning because many times you will find that you need specific material that you may have forgotten about. Don't assume that the student knows how to do any step in the process.

What Is Finished?

If possible, take a picture of what you expect the finished task to look like. If you expect students to "clean" up the bookshelves, first fix it the way you want it to look and take a photo of it. Then, at a later time, when you need it to be "cleaned," you can show them the picture of what you expect it to look like when finished.

Organization

All students need to learn this because they are not born with this skill. If you want a three-ring binder organized a certain way, have a sample made up with specific dividers that you require. Give ten minutes at the end of the week for students to put papers in the right sections. Most students are guilty of saying they will get to it later, so let them know that "later" has arrived.

Behavior

Look beyond the misbehavior and try to find the cause. Many times the misbehavior is due to anxiety. The student may be anxious about transitioning to a new activity or because they don't understand the assignment. They may be anxious about the noise level or activity going on around them. Once you find out the cause of the problem, it is easier to address the behavior.

Movement

Some students need movement in order to focus. Students may need wiggle chairs or to squish Nerf balls or twist rubber sticks. Some students may need to pace in the back of the room in order to focus on what you are saying. Don't try to contain these students in a chair and expect them to learn.

The beginning of the year is a good time to bring this to your students' attention. When explaining why some students are allowed to do this and others are not, I like to compare it to eating foods. Some people need different foods for a variety of reasons. Some may not be allowed to have sugar while others may need to have some other kind of food. Everyone's dietary needs are different. The same principle applies to the classroom. Everyone may need different strategies to succeed.

Assessments

Rather than long writing assignments, give fill-in-the-blank questions or multiple choice. You may need to try different alternative assessments that will work for the individual student. Some examples may be having a student make a book cover for an imaginary book on the topic they learned or making a movie poster about the topic.

Emotions

Students with autism may have trouble reading others' emotions—their body-language cues or facial expressions. Sarcasm can be especially difficult to understand, so avoid this as much as possible. Don't assume that a student will know you are happy or mad. Always let them know how you are feeling if it is important to you to convey this to them. Help them learn how to read other people's cues.

Social Stories

These are stories that help students learn how to behave in specific situations that they are having difficulty handling. Pick a specific behavior you want them to learn and write a personal story for them. Use their name and picture if possible. Specifically, state the actions of others and how they should respond appropriately. This social story is something they can refer to often when they need a reminder of how they should act. Once they accomplish one behavior, you can write a new story for another behavior that they need to work on. They may need several social stories made throughout the year. For smaller children, you can make this social story into a flip book for them. Older students may only need the story written out on a sheet of paper.

Making Friends

Students with autism can sometimes have trouble making friends. You might ask some of your particularly empathetic students to take turns buddying up with the student at lunch. Sometimes you might find an older student from another class who could be a "buddy" to them at lunch or at other times they might cross paths. If you work at a secondary school, you might talk to an athletic coach about trying to use some of the athletes as mentors for your students.

Meltdown or Tantrum?

Sometimes it is hard to distinguish whether the student is having a meltdown or just a childish tantrum. When having a tantrum, they are looking for a reaction and can usually tell you what they want. If they can control their behavior because they know they are causing an unsafe situation, they are having a tantrum. If whatever is making them mad is removed and they calm down, they are having a tantrum. Usually, students having a meltdown can't control their behavior even if what they are doing is unsafe. They can't tell you what is upsetting them, and even if you think you have fixed the problem, they don't calm down. Other teachers may comment that they don't understand why you allow your students to have tantrums. They may see these students as spoiled and undisciplined. You may have to explain that they were not having a tantrum but instead having a meltdown, which is completely different.

When this happens, giving the student a weighted blanket or vest may help calm him down. Putting on headphones with calming music may help. Letting them do their own calming ritual at this time should be allowed. While the student is working through the meltdown, move your other students to an area where they are safe if necessary. Eventually other students will be used to this behavior and continue to work on their assignments.

Noise

Many students with autism are sensitive to noise levels. A lot of noise is distracting and can cause them actual pain. They can be sensitive to loud noises such as fire alarms or school assemblies. These are good opportunities to teach coping skills for these situations. Outside of school, noisy situations may occur, and the student will need to know some solutions to deal with them.

Consider having the student wear noise-canceling headphones when the alarm goes off. Review the emergency procedures with this student often and explain that it is important to follow these procedures for everyone's safety. Explain that you know there will be a situation that will seem chaotic for this student, but it will be okay. You might also assign another student to be this student's "buddy" during an evacuation, which may help keep him calm.

During school assemblies, ask if the student can go to an alternate location such as the library or the nurse's office if the noise gets to be too much for this student. The student may also put on headphones or earbuds to lessen the noise.

Allow students to wear noise-canceling headphones or earplugs while they do their individual work, and this will help them stay focused on their work.

Learning Disabilities

Many of the following strategies work for all students with disabilities and others may work better for a specific student. You will need to try different ones with different students to find out what works to meet the needs of the individual. There is no magic wand that will work the same for everyone. This is the hard work of teaching, but when you find a strategy for a student that faces a lot of challenges and they begin to learn, the payoff, both for you and them, is immense.

Daily Schedules

Daily agendas will also help students with learning disabilities. These are usually in the form of a pocket calendar or a notebook calendar. They help students keep track of what they need to do and when it needs to be done. Time management may be a struggle for some, especially when there is a deadline to turn in an assignment. You will need to help them develop the practice of writing assignments and their due dates into their agenda. Then you will need to help them learn to check the agenda daily to stay on track with their assignments.

Projects that need to be worked on over time must be broken down into smaller steps. Each step may need to be completed on a specific date. All of these completed steps will form the final project.

Any changes in the schedule should be shared in advance with the student if possible. You will notice when the routine is changed, the students will be thrown off course and it may affect them the rest of the day.

Organizational Skills

Organization is a common struggle and needs to be taught. Don't just tell students that they need to be organized. Show them how to organize their work. Even take photos of it when it is organized the way it should be. Then the students can refer back to the photos if needed. Make sure you give them time to organize their work.

Have them keep a three-ring binder with their work organized. At the front of the binder, have them create an index so they can look at the separate sections to know where to put specific work.

Help students look for patterns which will help them learn to organize. Give them items and have them organize them into groups. Then have them explain why they grouped them that way. Different students may have these items grouped in different ways, which is okay as long as they can explain their reasoning behind the groupings.

Assignments

You should break long assignments into smaller ones, so they are not overwhelming. Depending on what type of learning disability the student has, you need to look at what accommodations and modifications need to be made to meet their needs. The student may get overwhelmed or frustrated on an assignment, and it would be beneficial to take a break from whatever is causing this problem and come back to it later. When the student has taken a break and is calmer, it may be easier to work through the problem.

Assessments

You may have to think of alternate assessments for this student to show understanding of the material. Know the student's strengths and allow the student to use this strength to show mastery of the material. If creativity is a strength, let the student make a poster or create something.

Misbehavior

Students with learning disabilities may act out as a defense mechanism. They don't want their peers to know that they can't do something. They would rather be known as the class clown instead of the class idiot. If this happens, meet with the student privately. Try to get to the cause of the misbehavior. You may even have to suggest that you think the student is acting out because of the fear of what other students may think of him. Suggest that he can give you a signal when he feels confident answering a question and that you won't call on him unless he gives you this agreed-upon signal. This will take some of the pressure off of him, and he may behave better during class.

Going Above and Beyond

One year I had two students who were doing a work internship at a local nursing home. Staff and residents loved them so much that they helped them go to the prom that spring. They all chipped in to buy prom tickets, rent the boy a tuxedo, buy the girl a gown and shoes, arranged for a reservation at a fancy Italian restaurant, along with a gift card to pay for it. One of the nurses had the evening off and was going to play their chauffeur to the restaurant and then to the dance. When I heard about these generous gifts, I knew my students well enough to know that they would be unable to navigate the process of eating in a fancy restaurant. I asked the young couple if they would mind if my husband and I joined them for dinner and both of them were so relieved that they quickly agreed. We were able to double date with them for the prom and everything went smoothly. They were unable to read the menu, so my husband pretended not to have his glasses and I was able to offer food suggestions for everyone. Both students watched what we did and imitated our actions during the dinner. Even though I took my own personal time to support the students, it was well worth it when I saw the joy on their faces at the end of the night.

Intellectual Disabilities

Students with intellectual disabilities usually have an IQ of seventy or below and deficits in adaptive functioning (such as functional life skills). People with traumatic brain injuries may experience the same characteristics.

Directions

Don't give too many directions at one time. Allow the student to complete a couple of steps before moving on to the next one. Make sure that the student understands the directions, and if they don't, try to give them directions in a different way. They may need to see you model it first in order to be able to do something. They may also need practice in order to do something independently.

Behavior

Like all students, students with intellectual disabilities respond well to praise. Most students want to please the teacher, and love to be helpers. They may get upset about things they don't understand or may misinterpret events and actions, so you will need to be patient and ask questions about why they are upset. They will respond better to positive than negative reinforcement.

Sometimes students can be very stubborn, especially when they get frustrated. When this happens, it is best to take a break and do something positive before coming back to tackle the difficult task.

Make sure you hold these students to high standards. Don't let them use their disability as an excuse not to do things you know they are capable of doing. Your belief in them will give them the confidence to learn more even though they will struggle.

Schedules

These students may benefit from visual schedules and daily agendas. It may be difficult for them to remember when assignments are due, and having them written down will help. You should teach them to check their agendas every day in order to develop this habit. Have them check the agenda before they leave your class, so they will know what assignment deadline is coming up.

Assignments

You should break down the tasks into steps. Assignments should be short and achievable. Long assignments will be overwhelming and cause frustration. If you do have a long assignment, try to break it up into smaller parts and have the student work on one part at a time. If students have success with one part, it will give them the confidence to do the next part.

Assessments

Assessments should not be too lengthy. It is best to give an assessment on the mastery of several steps before teaching new steps. This ensures that the student understands the smaller steps. After mastery of the smaller steps, you can have them put all of the steps together for the final assessment.

Making Friends

Students with intellectual disabilities sometimes will want to be friends with everyone, which can make them vulnerable. They may need guidance in making the right choices about their friends. There should be plenty of discussion about what makes a good friend and how they show it. Explain the difference between making friends who are good for you and those who may get you in trouble. This will take a lot of patience because they will insist that no one would want to be a bad influence on them.

Support

There may be times that these students will need extra support and they won't know to ask for it. Be aware of the activities they are involved in and prepare them ahead of time for any obstacles they may face. You may even have to spend some personal time helping them, but that is a decision you will have to make depending on the circumstances.

Paraprofessionals

At some point, you might have a paraprofessional in your classroom, especially if you are a special-education teacher. As a general-education teacher, you might have a paraprofessional assisting a student with special needs in your classroom. If you do have someone like this in your room, you are usually considered their immediate supervisor.

It is up to you to let the paraprofessionals know what is expected of them. Having a list of duties that you both sign off on helps clarify all the expectations. (For an example of this kind of list, see Appendix II at the back of the book.) It is also important to know how you will handle any disagreements between both of you. Decide if you will meet at the end of the day to go over the day or weekly to summarize the week. This will allow you learn what changes you might need to make. The paraprofessional may have some suggestions or may be able to tell you if something is not working. A paraprofessional is a great resource to have in the classroom. It is also important to make sure you often let the paraprofessional know how much you appreciate their hard work. Most paraprofessionals don't get paid a lot but are there because they love to work with students. Getting appreciation can go a long way.

Sometimes a paraprofessional is there as support for a special-education student during a general-education class. If this is the case, you should meet with this person and the special-education teacher to determine the expectations for the paraprofessional. Do you mind if the paraprofessional helps other students if students ask them for help? Does the paraprofessional feel comfortable helping other students? Is it okay for the paraprofessional to help hand out papers or not? Will this person sit beside the student they are there to help or at the back of the room? In what way will the paraprofessional help the student they are assigned to? It is better to have these expectations determined beforehand so no one gets their feelings hurt or people assume others are going to do things that they don't want to do.

Being the Boss

My first teaching job was in a self-contained classroom and I had a paraprofessional in my classroom. Since I had never taught before, it was hard for me to wrap my head around being someone's immediate supervisor. I found out at the end of the year that I was expected to evaluate her, which was intimidating for me since she had more classroom experience than I did! Before the students arrived, I decided that we needed to make sure that we had a list of duties expected of her. I think she was relieved to know this as well as I was, so we sat down together and composed a list of duties. I also shared my behavior plan with her and explained that I expected her to be consistent and fair while enforcing the plan. Another thing we discussed was how we would handle any conflicts or disagreements we might have between us. I think this is always important to discuss before any problems arise, to determine the best procedure ahead of time. It's important to have every stakeholder in the classroom on the same page in front of the students, so they won't play them against each other.

In this chapter you learned about:

- Working with students who have autism
- Working with students who have learning disabilities
- Working with students who have intellectual disabilities
- Working with paraprofessionals in the classroom

CHAPTER EIGHT

Culturally Responsive Teaching Methods

When I was growing up on Long Island in the sixties, I was one of a small handful of Asian students at my school. There was one other Chinese family whose children attended my elementary school. I don't care what year it is or where you live, if you are different, kids will notice. During the times when schools want you to conform, it is really hard to appear physically different. This was during the Vietnam War, which was a hard time to be Asian. I grew up facing a lot of prejudice and bullying because I was different.

Teachers need to do a good job in the classroom to teach tolerance and acceptance of those who are different from us. We need to embrace the individuality and uniqueness of everyone. Students have enough to worry about in today's society. They shouldn't have to be worried because they are different. I am realistic that this won't happen overnight or in one class session. It may take years to teach young people to accept those who are different, but you have to start somewhere.

Acknowledging Differences

First, start by having students talk about how all people in the world are different from one another generally. Let them brainstorm and list the ways all people are unique. Encourage them not to make judgments of the differences but just observations. Usually, students will start off with physical differences, but they will eventually move on to cultural differences. There should be no bad or good statements about the differences. For many people, differences are not noticeable to them and

125

they may be surprised that they are to others. Some students may also mention things that no one even considered before. Brainstorming is a great way to bring a group together where they can share ideas without any judgment.

This discussion is a great way for students to learn that even though people may be different, they also are alike in some ways. Being different is not a bad thing, and rather than focusing so much on how people are different, we need to recognize how much people are alike. Between the ages of twelve and eighteen, students are searching for their identity. They work hard at being "like everyone else" and notice other students who are "different." This activity helps in showing that not everyone has to be alike and it is okay to be different.

Exploring Cultures and Religions

You should encourage students to learn about different cultures. I realized when I started traveling on cruise ships how interesting it was to learn about different cultures. The more I learned, the more interested I became. I believe that prejudice and intolerance happen because of people's lack of knowledge. It is human nature to be afraid of what we don't know, so to get rid of that fear, we need to help our students learn about others.

I like to survey the students and parents and ask them if they would like to share with the class their background or heritage. I still find it interesting that my own parents escaped from Communist China in 1949 with two small children. Some of these families may feel honored to be included in other students' learning experience. This would be a great time for families to share their traditions and even some of the foods they eat.

Having students do research about other cultures and religions and then sharing the information with the class can be powerful. During the sharing part, other students may even offer some of their personal experiences that they hadn't been willing to share before. This can be a non-threatening way for them to share information about their own cultures.

Being Sensitive to Religious Minorities

Different religions can also be a sensitive subject, especially if there is a minority group in the community. One year I had my class read the novel *Four Perfect Pebbles*. The author had been held in the same concentration camp as Anne Frank. I was able to contact the author and get her to come to our area to speak to our students. Instead of just inviting my class to hear her speak, I invited the whole school and community. The author spent a lot of time talking about her personal experiences and accepting others for who they are. I was surprised when we had the whole auditorium full. It was well received by all. Later, I had parents come up to me to thank me for inviting the community because there aren't many opportunities for our students to learn about the Jewish people. I was thrilled that they appreciated it so much.

Many schools don't teach geography as a separate class, so it is important to incorporate geography into your lessons. One way to do this is to study one place that students aren't familiar with at a specific time. Students can find the location on the map. Rather than just looking at pictures in books, find videos about the country. Try different recipes and bring in some food from that country. Find someone on Skype to connect with and have them visit your class online. Many stereotypes are discarded when students meet actual people from different places.

If you are reading a book and the location is a real place, have your students find the location on the map. Have them explore the climate and find images or videos of the area. This will help them relate better to the story.

For math, you can discover the distance between two locations. Or have students plan a trip and figure out the distance they will travel round trip. You can have the class plan a vacation, including how much it would cost to do the things they would want to do on the trip. This type of activity, which brings in the real world, will get students really engaged.

Learning from Others

One time I had my students talk to another class in Alaska and they learned that people in Anchorage don't live in igloos. They also learned about the Iditarod, sled dogs, and how daylight is affected by the different seasons. Students from Anchorage learned that my students don't live in run-down shacks without plumbing or walk barefoot all day long. It was enlightening for both groups who had a stereotype in their mind that was false. Students also learn about major holidays that are celebrated in other countries. By talking to other students, they learn about the local weather and landscape, too.

Respecting Disabilities

Some students may have disabilities that are not noticeable—or even diagnosed. Most students are aware of their own ability and can feel excluded from the class without knowing why. It is important that you make accommodations and modifications that are necessary for all students to feel included and never ashamed, especially if they have or you suspect they have a disability. It is important to ask the student for input if you have some question about what to do. Many of them are willing to share with teachers what they need but are never asked. Students with disabilities feel like they have such little control over their lives, and being asked for their input can be truly empowering for them.

To help engender respect, you can plan special lessons. I like to do a week that I call Exceptional Children's Week, in which the students do simulations as if they have different disabilities. They may have to wear a blindfold as if they were visually impaired and navigate obstacles around the room. They may have to sit through a lesson wearing noise-canceling headphones as if they are hearing impaired. We borrowed a wheelchair and let students change classes in it to understand the difficulties of being unable to walk. Some students had to write with their nondominant hand to understand what it is like to have dysgraphia. Others had to use a mirror and write letters as they looked in a mirror so they understood how hard it is to write things with dyslexia. Some students were even willing to talk about their own disabilities, the frustrations they feel, and what they wish others would know about their disability. One of my students talked about autism and how it made her act. She wanted people to know that it hurt her when they made fun of her and didn't want to be her friend. Then she said the thing she wished for most was to have a friend to sit with at lunch. The next day, I saw her at lunch with a few of her new friends and I was so proud of my other students for responding to her this way. After doing many of these activities, many of the students had a better understanding of the difficulties that others may face and were more patient and understanding of disabilities.

Understanding Nontraditional Families

Many students come from nontraditional families, and you need to be very careful not to make them feel excluded. Some students may come from single-parent families and others may have same-sex parents. You should especially keep a close eye on these students to make sure they are not bullied.

Storytelling is a great strategy to teach reading or social skills. Instead of using stories with traditional families involved, try to use books that use real or fictitious animals. I've used many Dr. Seuss and Winnie-the-Pooh books to teach social skills. A book I read to my class is *And Tango Makes Three* by Justin Richardson and Peter Parnell, about two male penguins who become partners and raise a penguin chick at the zoo. *Okin the Panda Bear Finds His Family* by Jeff Lutes is a fabulous book that talks about adoption, nontraditional families, diversity, and the deaf culture. These books keep the focus on the skill or idea that I'm trying to teach instead of any human characters in the story. There are plenty of books out there if you search for them. Taking the time to go through the children's section at the library is a great way to find these resources. Other teachers in your school might also have suggestions and can share their favorite books with you.

Overcoming Exclusion

Talk with your students about ways we all feel excluded sometimes and how that makes us feel. How do other people act that makes us feel bad? Do we ever act this way? How can we make others not feel excluded? What should we do when we see someone else being treated poorly?

Get the students to brainstorm ways to help include people and write them on the board. Sometimes seeing it and hearing it helps to remind them. If someone is new to the class or school, offer to help them if they need it. If students notice someone is alone at lunch, it would be nice to join them and talk to them. If students notice someone at recess that has no one to play with, invite them to join you in whatever you are doing. If students have to partner with someone in class and there is an odd number of people, invite a single person to join your group.

If someone is being treated poorly, suggest the students be supportive of that person. Stand near them so they won't feel alone. There is safety in numbers and, usually, when the person is not alone, others will stop harassing them. Tell them to stop treating others this way. Go tell a teacher if necessary.

Another important thing to teach students is that sometimes people perceive actions differently from the way the other person intended. Have students role-play situations where they say the same statements but change their facial expressions and body language to portray different emotions each time. Have the class share how they perceived what the student was saying and how it made them feel. Then talk about the words we use and how they can affect people in a positive or a negative way along with the tone of voice. Encourage students to share what they are feeling rather than assuming that others understand how they are feeling. People may misinterpret how others are feeling by misreading facial and body cues, but if the students state how they are feeling, others can understand it better.

I have seen many people deeply offended by someone else's actions but the other person in no way meant offense. Sometimes something a person says can trigger someone else. When I was younger, I was offended when a stranger came up to me and asked me where I was from. Looking back, I realize that I faced a lot of prejudice growing up and all I wanted to do was to be like everyone else and never would be. This question always brought up the fact that I looked different. I know the stranger who asked did not mean to be offensive and may have been truly curious or interested in my heritage, but I perceived it as offensive. Eventually, as I grew older, I realized that I needed to be proud of my heritage.

Make sure you are not excluding someone from any activity because of their gender. I have had some students told that they couldn't take a woodworking class because they were girls or boys couldn't take a consumer science class because only girls can take them. In younger classes, boys and girls can play with dolls and dress-up. Boys and girls can work with play construction tools. Don't pigeonhole children into roles according to their gender. Some students still grow up in families with this kind of bias, and even though they are no longer applicable in today's society, respect the family's opinions. We had one situation in a cooking class where a student refused to wash the dishes because in his culture only women did that job. We wanted to be understanding of his culture, but also explain that in this situation, men and women shared many responsibilities. We also need to be respectful of students who are dealing with their own gender issues and make sure they are not excluded from any activities.

Teaching Students to Handle Difficult Situations

One way to help students when they are confronted with bullying or insensitivity due to their race, religion, disability, or anything else that makes them feel separate from the mainstream is to role-play different situations. This is like having a fire drill and being prepared if there is ever a fire. You want your students to feel comfortable and know what to do if a situation ever arises where they feel like they should take some positive action. You don't want them to think they should do something and then not know what to do. The more they practice doing the right thing, the easier it will be to actually do this if they need to.

You can use some examples they gave about instances where they have felt or seen someone else excluded for some reason or another. Not only do you role-play the situation, but afterward you critique what happened. Do students think this was the right way to act? Are there other positive ways they can act? What if something else happens after they act? How will they handle that next situation? Ask a student to pretend they are sitting at lunch all alone, wishing they had a friend to talk to. Then ask other students to show how they would act if they saw this. Some may sit with that student and others may walk to another table. Then you can talk about the whole scene after it is finished and ask students why they acted that way and what else they could have done. You might suggest that they ask their friends to go sit with this person or invite that person to sit with them. Try to reenact a bullying situation and have students show what they would do or what they wish others would have done. Then talk about how they handled the situation or what they could have done differently. Talk about how other students can tell the bully to stop bothering the person because usually bullies pick on someone they think doesn't have anyone who will stick up for them. Recommend that students tell a teacher about the situation and stress that they should never react with violence. Reflecting on our actions is the most important part of learning.

In this chapter, you learned about:
- Acknowledging differences
- Exploring cultures and religions
- Teaching students to accept and respect people with disabilities
- Understanding nontraditional families
- Working with students to avoid exclusion
- Teaching students to handle difficult situations

CHAPTER NINE
Technology in the Classroom

It is important to remember that technology is just a tool and should not take the place of the teacher. There was no computer technology when I first started teaching, and while technology is great, many teachers expect too much from it. They depend on it and are under the false assumption that technology will make them great teachers. They act like technology is the magic pill that will fix all things and make the student instantly successful. Yet, if the student doesn't have the skills to learn and the ability to apply these skills, their knowledge of technology is useless.

How technology is used in the classroom is dependent on the situation. Some classes might only have a few computers in the room for all of the students to share, some schools supply each student with a device during the school year, and some schools allow students to bring their own devices. The rules for student use are also different among schools and districts, so it is important to know your district's technology policy.

No matter what the tech situation is at your school, it is important to teach responsible technology use. It is a tool that is needed as a job skill, so it is important that you teach students how to use it. A lot of old-school educators are resistant to technology in the classroom, but I'm sure some felt the same way when calculators were first used in the classroom and before long, graphing calculators were required in some classes. People felt this way when the first cell phones came on the scene too, and now everyone has one. When the first automobile was invented, no one would have imagined how vital it would become to many of our lives.

Like any other tool, technology can be used inappropriately by anyone. Pens and pencils can be used for classwork or for doodling instead of doing assigned tasks. Students learn to read, and we want them to read the appropriate material, but some may choose to read inappropriate things. We teach students to drive and we want them to drive safely and responsibly, but some may drive recklessly and carelessly. These are choices students make with the skills that they have acquired. It is important that we teach students that they have choices to make and how to make the right choices for the tools that they use.

Learning About New Tech

Attending technology conferences is extremely useful. This is a great time to learn about new devices, instructional strategies, and programs that will help your instruction. I like to learn about new things that have been developed that might help my students. Learning new strategies to use in the classroom is a great way to grow professionally. I have always learned something new at every conference that I have attended. Many school districts host a technology conference, or your state may host one. You may have to contact your district's instructional technology coordinator to find out when and where the nearest technology conference is held.

Appropriate Uses

Like any other tool, there is a time and a place when it is appropriate to use technology. Using individual devices while driving is never appropriate. Using them to cheat, lie, or hurt others is also never appropriate. Using them to socialize during class is a no-no. There is so much information out in the world about this that sometimes teachers don't address tech basics with their students, but this can never be stressed enough whenever it is possible.

At the beginning of the year, students and parents sign a Responsible Technology Use Form so they understand the rules before using any school technology devices. When you give an assignment that will require the use of a computer, it is important that you go over the ground rules with the students beforehand. When you ask the students to use the word processor, they should not be surfing the Web. Also, if you ask them to do some writing, they should not be copying and pasting someone else's work. If you ask them to go to specific websites, they should not be playing games on the computer or going to sites other than the one they are directed to. Many school districts have blocks on inappropriate websites, but if you see one not blocked, you need to make sure that is sent to the instructional technology director to be blocked.

Safety Issues

Teaching about Internet safety is also important. It is vital that students learn to never give out personal information over the Internet to anyone and definitely not on a public forum where anyone could see it. Again, you may think that others have stressed this with your students, but it never hurts to remind them until it becomes second nature. Even though there is so much information out in the world about this, children are still being exploited because of contact with inappropriate people over the Internet. Never worry about being too cautious. It is always better to be safe than sorry.

One rule of thumb to teach your students about posting on the Internet or on social media is that if they can't show it to their grandmother, then they shouldn't be doing it online. They need to realize that their online presence can affect them later in life, whether with college applications or employment opportunities. Many colleges and employers are looking at candidates' online activities to decide if they are a good fit for them. Once it is online, it is impossible to erase, so this rule of thumb helps students make smart decisions about their actions online.

Communication

Technology is a great way to communicate with others. It gives you several different options, and you need to find the one that works for you.

I like calling parents over the phone often and even giving them my personal phone number. I always felt like communication was a two-way street, so if I had their phone number, why shouldn't they have mine? It sets up an instant feeling of trust, which many have not felt toward the school before. This feeling helps them be more receptive to my ideas and discussions without feeling defensive. You should set up parameters though and ask them not to call before a certain time in the morning and after a certain time in the evening. If you don't feel comfortable giving out your personal phone number, use an Internet-based phone number such as the ones offered by Google Voice so you can give out a contact number other than your personal phone number. If someone calls this number, it forwards to your personal number and the other party never sees your personal number.

Emailing others helps you keep documentation about your communication. Remember that if you send a group email, it is better to put all of the email addresses in the blind copy address bar (bcc:). If you don't, everyone you send the email to has everyone else's email address, and some parents don't want their email address given out.

There are plenty of apps that will let you text parents or even groups of people such as a group of students or colleagues. There is an app called Remind that allows you to text a group such as parents about events or activities that are going on in your classroom. You can also send a message to your students reminding them about an assignment or a test that is coming up. For real-time communication, this is better than sending out an email. With Remind, you can schedule announcements in advance. Remind has a limited free account, but some school districts have paid to upgrade, so check if it or a similar app is available in your school district. Remind is just one example of an app you can use. There are others, such as GroupMe and TextPlus, so you can experiment to see what platform you like best. I'm sure there are even more. You just need to find the one that works the best for you and meets your needs.

Behavior Tracking

Using an Excel spreadsheet is a great way to keep frequency charts on student behaviors. Some behaviors to track are not following directions, not paying attention, calling out and disrupting the class, getting out of their seat without permission, calling others' names, touching others, and not completing assigned tasks. By doing this instead of handwriting this information, you don't have to worry about losing it. If you need to email it to a psychologist, administrator, or parent, it will be easier to read than a handwritten chart. The main thing you have to remember is to give a key to any abbreviations or symbols that you use. Today, there are many online tools that help you track behavior. Some teachers use a free app called ClassDojo with a lot of success in managing students' behaviors. It is time-consuming, but many feel it is worth the effort to improve behaviors in class.

Games as Rewards

Using devices to play games can also be a great reward for appropriate behavior. I just make sure that the games that are available are learning games. If the students have completed reading assignments, I let them play reading games. If they have completed math assignments, I let them play math games. I usually bookmark the sites in a folder on the browser so they are easily found. This way students won't have to try to type in any long Web addresses in the address bar. If they type one wrong letter, they won't get to the right place and this will lead to a lot of wasted time and frustration. It also keeps them from being distracted and going to other sites.

Behavior Frequency Chart

Behavior observed: Getting out of seat without permission
Frequency: 2-minute intervals
(Mark if observed)

Date:	10/20/18	10/21/18	10/22/18	10/23/18	10/24/18
0					
2					
4					
6	X	X	X	X	X
8					
10					
12		X			X
14				X	
16	X		X		X
18					
20		X			
22					
24	X		X	X	
26					X
28					
30			X		
32					
34					
36					
38	X	X	X	X	X
40	X	X	X	X	X
42					
44					
46	X	X	X	X	X
48					
50	X	X	X	X	X
52	X	X	X	X	X
54	X	X	X	X	X
56					
58	X	X	X	X	X
60					

Teaching Websites and Apps

The great thing about the information on the Internet is that it makes teaching easier today than when there was no Internet. There are a lot of resources teachers can gain access to easily, but they have to take the time to look for them. Many websites offer lesson plans to go along with their information, which can be modified and adjusted for your needs.

There are so many educational apps and websites that enhance instruction in all sorts of subjects—language arts, math, science, social studies, and even fine arts lessons. Others may teach career exploration or functional living skills. There are also some that help students learn a foreign language. I do not believe that these things can replace instruction in a classroom because a teacher can read body language and facial expressions of students where a device is not able to do so. If the student is confused or frustrated, a teacher can tell this when a device can't. It is easy for a student to guess and hit the right key in order to get a correct answer, but a teacher is able to see if the student understands or is just guessing. Technology is great for information, enhancing initial instruction, and practice, but it's just one piece of the overall picture of education.

Websites as Resources

There is plenty of information out there about different topics, but it is important that as teachers, we verify that the information students are getting from websites is legitimate. There is a lot of misinformation and inaccurate information that anyone can put up on the Web, and we need to teach students how to judge the information they are getting. We need to teach critical thinking skills so that they don't automatically believe everything they read and see. Have students get information from a website and determine who the author is. If no author can be determined, don't count it as a reliable site. When was this information written? If no date can be determined, you have no way of knowing how current this information is. What is the website's purpose? Is this a commercial site promoting their own product or are they giving an opinion of something? If they give facts and figures, they need to investigate how the author came up with these figures. Did they get them from specific research or make up this information? If they got this from specific research, who did the research, when was the research done, and was this research from a reliable source?

If you are sending students to specific websites, make sure you check out the sites before your lesson. Make sure the Web address that you are giving students works correctly. You would hate to give the wrong address and have the students end up at an inappropriate site. If you are asking students to find answers to questions, make sure they are able to find the answers where you want them to look. Nothing is more frustrating to discover that the answers you were expecting them to find aren't there. You will waste too much precious time trying to help them and then redirecting them to other places.

Educational Videos

Educational videos are also a great teaching tool for your class. There are plenty of educational videos on YouTube if you search for them. Ted-Ed talks are always quality videos, and you might find some that would be good to introduce a lesson that you are teaching. YouTube has tons of videos for you to use for your class. Just put the topic your class is studying in the search bar and you will get the list of videos to choose from. Try to access the video from your school computer to make sure that this online video is not blocked by your district. If it is blocked and you still want to show it, contact your instructional technology person to see what process you need to go through to get it unblocked. Preview all videos before showing them to your class. Create some questions for your students that go along with the videos in order to help them focus on the content.

File Storage and Sharing

Cloud storage such as Google Drive can be useful to store files so that you can access them on any device. Students sharing their Google Drive folders means you don't have to worry about attachments on emails or someone forgetting to send a file to you. It also ends the excuses of "I sent it to you, but I don't know why you didn't get it!" The other good thing about sharing folders is that if someone else accidentally deletes a file, there should be a record of this action, so you would know who did it and even find the lost file. There are other online storage platforms, such as Dropbox or OneDrive. The main thing to impress upon students is to be careful who they share the link to their folders with.

Copyright and Plagiarism

Teaching students about copyright is important. Even some adults don't understand how this works. Explain to your students that they can use pictures they personally take, or those that don't have a copyright restriction on them (e.g., images in the public domain), or images that allow for educational use in their copyright statement. This is a good time to explain Creative Commons to them. Other good sites like Pixabay or Unsplash have free pictures for you to use. The same rules apply to music also.

A Creative Commons license is something that creators give people certain rights to use and share the work that they have created as long as credit is given to the creator. Depending on the type of license, they may be allowed to use the work "as is" for commercial or noncommercial use or let others edit the work for noncommercial and/or commercial use.

It is important to teach students that using anything without the creator's permission may be an infringement of copyright laws and should not be done. Also, knowingly using someone else's words and passing them off as your own is plagiarism, which is definitely not tolerated in the classroom. Many instances of plagiarism, especially in the higher grades, are treated as cheating and addressed in a meeting with the student, parents, and administration.

The Magic of Scrapbook Pages

For assessments, Photoshop or Photoshop Elements are good tools to teach students how to do digital scrapbooking. This is a great way to encourage students to create something to show what they have learned. Again, this cuts down on any cheating students might tempted with on a written test. There is a learning curve, so I would suggest that you figure out how to do this before showing students. Once you know how to do a simple scrapbook page, write up the directions so students can follow the sequential steps easily. (See page 172 for my instructions.) At first, have everyone make the same page so they can all learn and practice the same skills. They need to learn how to find pictures and save them in a specific folder so they can find them again. Once they've mastered the skills, they are ready to make their own pages.

This activity could be used for any topic, whether it is language arts, a math concept, or even a social studies or science topic. Once the students have completed their research, have them draw a rough draft of how they want their scrapbook page to look. This is called creating a storyboard. They can draw shapes where they want the pictures and text to go. This could be revised once they begin working on the computer because they might want to change parts of it, but having an idea is a good starting point. At first this is a slow process because it is new to the students. After they have done this several times, it gets easier. Encourage students to help one another rather than always depending on you for help. Sometimes their peers can explain things easier to them or they might not get as defensive as they would with you because they think you might be criticizing them.

After students complete their scrapbook page, have them share it with the class. They may present it on a screen digitally or they may print it out. Ask them why they chose the pictures they used and have them share their research. As students get used to this activity, it is amazing to watch them explore and try new skills to make their scrapbook pages fancier or more appealing. They no longer want the basic page. This is the time to have them look at magazines for page-design elements. Have them look at why a page appeals to them and have them try to apply the same principles to their pages. The more appealing the page, the more interested the observer is about learning the information on the page.

Never forget to have them reflect on and evaluate their work. Did they accomplish their goal? Was the audience reaction as expected? What did they like about the project and why? What would they do differently and why? This kind of reflection is great to use for every project, and once it becomes a habit, it will be easier. This is an important step in learning. Without this, we all just keep repeating the same mistakes.

Blogging

Blogs are multifaceted in that you can read them, write your own, and have students keep them. They serve a lot of different purposes. Teachers may read blogs in order to get new ideas and to connect with other teachers. They may write their own to share their thoughts and ideas and to reflect on their own teaching methods. Students may write a blog to share with others what activities are happening in the classroom or special events that have happened in the school. They also can share their opinions or feelings with others. This is a good way for students to share information they have learned about a specific unit, a field trip, or from a visiting speaker.

Teacher Blogs

I have been blogging for thirteen years now and I still love it. There has been a lot of discussion about whether blogging has become obsolete, and I don't think it has if you are using it for reflection and connection. I think it is a great way to make writing relevant and improve your reading and writing abilities.

I like to blog about a lesson in order to reflect on my teaching habits. I explain the lesson I taught, how the students did with the activity, what went well, what didn't go well, and what I would do differently. Sometimes it is hard to remember how the lesson went months later, and I can look back at this to help me with a similar lesson, or if I want to repeat the lesson the next year, I have a reference to use so the lesson could be better. I might forget that something sounded like a good idea but when I had the students do the activity, it was a flop. Rather than repeat the same mistake, I can look back at my blog post and remember what I need to change this time. I believe it is this reflection that helps teachers be more effective.

Sharing a link to my blog with others on social media encourages others to read my posts. Many times they offer suggestions that I hadn't thought about and want to try. Sometimes I give other people new ideas that they want to try in their classrooms.

Blogging is also a great way to post a question or a problem and have the online community help you. Sometimes I have struggled with an obstacle when wanting to teach a specific lesson and I explain the problem in my blog. This has opened doors to resources and solutions to the problem because people from different perspectives see the problem in other ways.

Sometimes if I'm having problems with helping a student succeed, I explain my problem. I share strategies I have tried that haven't worked. I might even share some of the suggestions that the parents have given. Someone who has dealt with a similar problem might read my post and have other suggestions that have worked for them.

Through my blog, I have met a lot of other teachers and students who agree and disagree with what I write. It has opened up a dialogue about some topics and encouraged further discussion. Blogging has helped me clarify my thoughts and better communicate my opinions. I believe it is important to comment on other people's blogs as well as reply to comments on my blog. This helps keep the connection with other people. It is a wonderful experience when I have been able to meet some of my online blogging friends in real life or on Skype.

I love to read blogs by other educators. Their recommendations help me find sites that may be useful to me, so I don't have to waste time looking at ones that aren't very good. You can get great new ideas for strategies to use in the classroom. I get excited when I find something new that might motivate my students or make learning fun. By reading other blogs, you might learn about a new technology or software that has been developed and whether it is worth using in the classroom. This also keeps you aware of current trends in education as well as new research that has been developed.

I use a free online aggregator called Feedly (feedly.com), which shows me at one time all of the blogs that I follow and any updates to the blogs.

This saves me time from going to each individual blog in order to see if they have updated it. Once I find a blog I like, I just add the address to the page. When the new posts are published, they will appear on this page. I can adjust the settings to preview a bit of the post so I know if I want to go to it and read more. Or I can click on it to show I read it. I can also bookmark it to read it later.

If you're interested in keeping your own blog, scheduling is something to think about. I like to write a post daily from Monday through Friday. I take the weekends off because I don't want to burn out. There are several free blogging platforms out there. Some school districts have their own platform that they want teachers to use. I like to use Blogger, but another popular platform is Wordpress.

Confidentiality Is Key

Confidentiality is extremely important when working with students and schools. When blogging, I never use a student's name or give out my school's name. Just like we teach our students Internet safety, it is vital when dealing with students to keep things confidential. I don't want anyone to come back with a lawsuit for breaking confidentiality laws or claim that I put any student in danger.

Student Blogs

Blogging is a great way to get students to write. Instead of useless paragraphs that many don't see as relevant, blogging can be personal and relevant to many students. It is a great way for students to have a voice and share their opinions and feelings. They can learn to use critical thinking when reading news stories and then write their opinions about them in their blog. They can write about something new they learned so they will remember it. Blogs can also be used as journals for students to write about their day, the high or low points of their days, and what they are feeling.

In addition, blogging can help with behavior issues. Some students who get angry easily are calmer after writing about their anger. Those who are depressed seem to feel better after blogging. Some shy students really blossom through blogging. Sometimes they get outshined by the louder, more outgoing students, and this is a way for them to safely stand out and be recognized. Blogs can even help students connect with others around the world who are like-minded.

Students can be required to write a post at least once a week but can write as often as they want to—as long as they have completed the one required post. Some students write every day and others two or three times a week.

You can adjust the privacy settings so that the student blogs are not open to the public and only people who have the link to the site can access the blog. Then you can send the link to parents and school personnel. You should also make sure that all comments have to be approved by you before getting posted on the blog, which protects any inappropriate comments from appearing.

Global Connections

As we grow up, we are egocentric. I didn't realize until I started blogging how egocentric I still am. When teachers from around the world started commenting on my blog and connecting with me, I realized that I had to look at my teaching differently. The world really is a smaller place when technology is involved. Not only was there a time difference but also seasonal differences and cultural differences. I would get questions about certain holidays, routines, and even terminology that was specific to where I lived.

Skype is a great way to connect with other teachers on your grade level or about your subject area around the world. Through these connections, you can get inspired by new strategies and discover new ways to engage your students in the classroom. One strategy I used was to connect with a class from another country and have the students learn how we are similar and how we are different. This led to exploring different cultures and religions that the students were unfamiliar with. When we talked with the other class, my students had great questions to ask the other students and they had many great questions for my students. Learning firsthand from other students was much more meaningful to my students than reading about the other country in a textbook. We actually had to schedule a second call at a later time to get all of the questions answered.

Don't Get Lost in Translation

Different terminology can be offensive in other parts of the world. I was shocked to learn that some common words we use here in the United States can be considered profanity in other parts of the world. When I was online, chatting with a class from another country about my state of South Carolina, I was sharing about our state symbols. I talked about our state bird, tree, flower, and fish. When I mentioned that our state dance was the shag, I heard an audible gasp from the class. It is not a word allowed in their classroom because it is considered profanity. You might want to do a little research about this topic before you hop online with a class in another country.

Another fun activity is a Mystery Skype call. Students connect with someone or another class and ask questions to guess where the other person or group is from. This is a great way to learn about geography and other cultures. Students can learn that classes around the world are similar to or different from the one they are in. It is a great learning experience for students and teachers! Skype in the Classroom, hosted by Microsoft is a free community that teachers can join. This is a great resource to find guest speakers for your class, find other classrooms around the world to connect with, or collaborate with others on a project.

This is useful when students are reading a book that is set in another country or focuses on another culture. Students might read about a holiday or a specific location that interests them. You can find other teachers or classes from that country or culture that would be willing to give firsthand knowledge to your students. This would make the learning experience so much richer and relevant to all of the students!

Look at the Time

I wasn't concerned with time differences from other countries because I didn't do a lot of real-time communication. Then one day I was contacted by a teacher in Australia. Her students were reading a book that was set in my state and talked about peach stands, but her students didn't know what a peach stand was. So my husband and I went out one day and took as many pictures as we could of different peach stands in the area. I sent the pictures to the teacher, who put them up on their class site. Then they contacted me again and asked if I could Skype with the class to talk about where I lived and how the election process worked in my country. I agreed to do this but then found out that their class met at the time I'm usually in bed fast asleep. So I got up around three a.m. and dressed like I was going to talk to a school class. We had a fascinating discussion! Those students were extremely excited to talk to me and ask questions. I was excited about how much I learned from them when we were comparing things from our countries. I really encourage other teachers to connect globally because it is a fabulous learning experience for all!

Other platforms that you can use to connect globally with educators are Twitter and Facebook. Usually, bloggers will give their contact information on their page with Twitter and Facebook links. From these feeds, you can look at the friends they have and some of the posts that their friends make. If you like their educational posts, you can request to follow them and make a connection with them. You can make many valuable online educator connections this way.

In this chapter, you learned about:
- Using technology appropriately in the classroom
- Managing safety issues
- Communicating through email, texts, and online
- Using spreadsheets to track behavior
- Teaching websites and apps
- Using websites as resources and teaching students what makes a site a good source
- Finding quality educational videos
- Using file storage and sharing
- Teaching students about copyright and plagiarism
- Scrapbooking as a tool for learning
- Blogging both for teachers and students
- Connecting to classrooms around the globe

CHAPTER TEN
Parent Involvement

Your relationship with the parents of your students is vital to a student's success in the classroom. The teacher, the parents, and the student make up a team, and their goal is to help the student succeed in your class.

Don't judge others until you have heard both sides of the story! I remember when I first started teaching and I thought I was going to change the world. I'm almost embarrassed just thinking about it. I thought every misbehaved child was just misjudged and not loved. I believed that with my love and instruction, every child was going to do wonderfully in the classroom. Boy, was I wrong! Sometimes it felt like no matter what I did, the students continued to struggle. They told me horror stories about their home lives and it broke my heart. Then I visited homes and met parents and the stories just didn't ring true. I realized that the students were just playing me and most of the students came from decent homes. In all my years of teaching, I've never met a parent who really didn't care about their child.

When I became a parent, I realized that children sometimes lie to get their way. Luckily I discovered this early in my teaching career, and that is why it is so important to have a relationship with parents. I realized that I shouldn't believe half of what I was told about the parents and, hopefully, they wouldn't believe half of what they were told about me!

Of course, I'm not talking about abuse cases, but rather the stories about how mean their parents are and that they don't get to do anything at home or that they can do anything they want because their parents don't care. These students are probably telling the same stories at home about how mean I am and that they don't get to do anything in class or that they can do anything in my class because I don't care. It is better not to judge parents from what the students are saying and to make your own judgments after you have worked with the parents over time.

A Team Effort

One part of the student-parent-teacher team is not better than the other. They all bring essential strengths to the table. I have had a lot of parents feel intimidated by teachers over the years, and I always want to put them at ease when I meet them. The teacher is viewed as the expert in education, but the parents are such a great resource for helping to motivate the student. The parents know certain strategies that will or won't work to help the student, and this keeps the teacher from wasting time on things that won't work. When you meet with parents, remind them that they are the true experts on their child and how important they are to your work with their child. Acknowledging the important role they play really puts them at ease. Some parents feel that because you have a college degree and they may not, you are smarter than them. This is not the case. It only shows that you have more knowledge about the classroom than they do.

The student should have input because when they feel they have a say in their instruction, they are more interested in succeeding. If there are issues, the team can meet to come up with solutions that may help the problem. No one needs to feel like they are trying to solve everything by themselves.

Making Contact

Every year I make sure that the lines of communication between the parents and myself are open. As a parent myself, nothing is more frustrating than contacting the teacher and not getting a response! After speaking with an attorney who specializes in education law, I learned that the biggest cause of complaints and lawsuits is that the parents feel they get no response from the school when contacted. It might take only a return phone call or email to make a parent feel like their concerns are being heard!

Since communication is such a key component to a good relationship with parents, as I've said earlier, at the beginning of the year I call all of the students' parents and introduce myself to them. I give a quick overview of my class, let them know I'll be calling them regularly to update them on their child's progress at school, and then I give them my phone number. I ask them not to call after eight p.m. and before seven a.m. I know many teachers are concerned about giving their personal phone numbers out. I've never felt that way because I tell the parents that we are a team. If I have their personal numbers, I am willing to give them mine. This instills a sense of trust between us. If teachers don't want to give out their own number, they can always set up an Internet phone number by using a service like Google Voice (see page 136 for more information). In more than thirty years, I've had only one parent who didn't follow that rule. I let the call go to voicemail, but I did call the parent back the next day. Some parents prefer email, and some prefer phone calls. When you first make contact, find out which they prefer.

I want to break the negative cycle of parents hearing from the school only when their child misbehaves or is having a problem, so when I first reach out to parents, I let them know that I will call them frequently to give them updates on their child. Usually, the first two phone calls are about the wonderful things that the student is accomplishing. This sets up future phone calls because the parents feel that I really care about their child and want them to succeed. If I have to call about a negative issue, they are more open to listening to me.

To keep these lines of communication open, I make a schedule where I divide the number of students up over ten days (two weeks of school days) and I contact that number of parents each day either by email or phone. I don't have to spend a lot of time with this once I have established regular contact with the parents. Parents appreciate knowing that they will be hearing from me often.

Positive Reports

This regular communication with parents will help tremendously with the discipline in your class. In the beginning, your students may not be used to having positive phone calls home. When you call home with your regular report and have positive things to say, ask the parents to let their child know that you were bragging about them. When the student returns to class, they will feel proud and try to act appropriately so you will call and brag about them again. Some of the other students may even ask why you haven't called their homes and you can ask them if they have done positive things for you to brag about. Usually they haven't, and you can tell them that if they act appropriately, you will call their homes that week. This helps them do better in class and you can call home to reinforce their good behavior. This positive cycle is so much better than a negative one.

Many of the parents I contact are not expecting any positive phone calls. Many have told me that they hear from the school only when their child is in trouble. I have had parents break down in tears when I have called to brag about their child, and one parent told me that this was the first time in ten years they heard anything good about their child. This broke my heart, and I pledged to make sure they heard more good things about their child. I know that being told constantly that your child is acting up in school can be disheartening and can actually impact family dynamics. This causes the parents to scold and punish the child, which doesn't always help the child improve their behavior. Without getting any feedback about whether the child's behavior improves or not, that may be the end of that situation for the family and it was a negative one.

When you call the parents and brag about their child, don't forget to ask them to let the child know that you called and how glad you are that they did what they were supposed to do. You will know that the parent has done this when the student comes to school and tells the class about it or shares that they were rewarded because of the phone call. This makes the students want to continue to do well so that you will call home again and brag about them. It is amazing how heartwarming this simple act of communication can be and how it can transform your class.

Getting the Right Information

Sometimes I get incorrect or outdated contact information. Sometimes a student may give me a wrong number on purpose. The student knows that usually when a teacher calls home, it isn't a good thing. If the student can get away with giving the wrong information, nothing is reported to the parents and the parents think the school is uncommunicative. So I tell the students that if I can't reach a parent, I will need to make a home visit. This usually gets me current contact information.

Home Visits

Very rarely do I have to make a home visit, but if I do, I get a partner to go with me to the home. I never go alone. I make it a quick stop and explain that I have been unable to reach them by phone or email and would appreciate it if I had a way to contact them. I let them know that I like to brag about my students often, so I won't just be calling if I have a problem. They usually don't believe me until after the second or third contact. I have had students who thought I would not go to their houses and refuse to give me correct contact information. Imagine the surprise on some parents faces when I show up at their home and explain to them that I only had the contact information given to me by their child. Then I give them my contact information so that they can call or email me if they have questions. By my actions, they know that I want to help their child and have gone out of my way to make sure that we can work as a team. It is amazing how much of a difference this can make throughout the year when I need their support.

Reporting the Not-So-Good

Whenever you do have to make the phone call that you are having problems with the student, parents will be more receptive to what you have to say. They know that you have taken time to contact them about the positive stuff and they are realistic about their child, so they know that sometimes negative stuff might happen. When you explain about consequences or needing help with finding solutions, the parents are more supportive because of your previous communication with them.

Most parents want to support teachers but don't really know how to do so. If you have parents ask you what they can do at home to help correct the problem, ask them what kinds of things the student likes to do at home. These things can either be taken away one at a time if the student's behavior doesn't improve or increased if the student's behavior does improve. Make sure that you contact the parent in a few days to give feedback to see if this has helped or not. Without getting this feedback, the parent has no idea whether their support is helping or not, and this is a strong example for everyone to see how well teamwork can help the student. The more everyone works together, the easier it is for parents to give support when you need it.

Getting Ahead of Problems

One time we had a conference about a student and all his teachers attended the meeting. One of the teachers was having a lot of behavior problems with him and nothing the teacher did seemed to have an impact. The parent turned to the student and asked him why he had so many problems in this teacher's class but none in my class. He looked at his parent and exclaimed, "Well, Mrs. H. had your phone number on speed dial in her phone! If I cause trouble, she stops what she is doing and calls you. Then I know I'm in big trouble!"

This showed that the student could obviously control his own behavior but chose not to do this. I keep hearing from other teachers that they don't have time to do all these contacts with parents, but here is proof that it is worth the time. When you are contacting parents often, these phone calls or emails don't take that long and are well worth the effort. I believe we can take the time on the front end for preventative action or we will spend more time on the back end dealing with behavior problems. Either way, we are going to have to put in the time dealing with this student. Isn't it easier for all if we can be proactive rather than reactive?

I know it isn't always possible to prevent bad behavior, but nipping it in the bud keeps it from getting worse. Sometimes we have to ask ourselves why the student is acting in a certain way. If he is acting this way because of problems in class (struggling, bullying, or other issues), we need to figure out a way to help him with these issues and control his behavior.

Students might need to sit in a different area of the classroom away from others to calm down. Sometimes putting on headphones and listening to music might help a student calm down if he is angry. Sometimes a student gets frustrated with the work they are doing and I allow them to take a break from that problem and do something else. The more they try to work on a problem that frustrates them, the harder it seems to become. Taking a break helps them relax and come back later with a fresh perspective. I also encourage them to ask for help when they get frustrated and angry rather than let their anger fester, which could lead to worse behavior that they struggle to control.

Conferences

At the beginning of the school year, the school usually has an open house night where you meet the parents. This is a good time to introduce yourself, explain what your class is, and your grading procedures. Explain that you will be contacting them and ask that they verify their contact information before they leave. Do not go too much in depth after that because you usually don't have a lot of time at these meetings. If you're at an upper-level school, they usually have the parents follow their child's schedule and ring a bell so they can meet each teacher for ten minutes. This is a great time to answer any general questions. If parents want to know about their individual child, offer to set up a conference at a later time so that you will be able to give it all of your attention.

Building Awareness

Having students become aware of their own behavior helps them learn to control it better. I had one student who was not aware that he got out of his seat so much, so every time he was out of his seat without permission, I gave him a button. At the end of class, we recorded the number of buttons on a chart. The next day, he tried hard to have fewer buttons. By the end of the week, we could see on the chart whether he was improving and he had. This chart was a great visual motivator in learning to control his behavior. I have also used this technique in order to get a student to stay on task. For every five minutes the student was on task, she got a button. We kept the chart to show how many buttons she got each day. By having the visual motivator, she wanted more buttons the next day and was so proud when the chart showed an increasing number. The more she practiced staying focused on her tasks, the more work she was completing, and her grades improved. These charts are a great way to show parents their child's progress.

Behavior Frequency Chart

Behavior observed: Getting out of seat without permission
Frequency: 2-minute intervals
(Mark if observed)

Date:	10/20/18	10/21/18	10/22/18	10/23/18	10/24/18
0					
2					
4					
6	x	x	x	x	x
8					
10					
12		x			x
14				x	
16	x		x		x
18					
20		x			
22					
24	x		x	x	
26		x			x
28					
30			x		
32					
34					
36					
38	x	x	x	x	x
40	x	x	x	x	x
42					
44					
46	x	x	x	x	
48					
50	x	x	x	x	
52	x	x	x	x	
54	x	x	x	x	x
56					
58	x	x	x	x	x
60					

When to Call a Conference

You should set up a parent conference if you are having a major problem with the student that you haven't been able to resolve. By this time, you should have called home several times but still haven't been able to fix the problem. You should also check with the students' other teachers to see if they are having problems, too. Often you will find out that they are having problems as well. This is the time to schedule a conference with the parents, including an administrator, the other teachers, and possibly a guidance counselor.

You should also hold a conference if the student's grade is failing. By the time report cards come around, you should have notified the parents a few times that the student was not doing what is necessary to get a passing grade. This may be due to failing tests or not completing classwork or homework. A conference should be held to work out a plan that will help the student succeed in improving their class grade.

Preparing for a Conference

When you are going to a conference, you should have a full "picture" of the student at the ready. Have a file on every student in your class. Keep any papers that you needed signed in this file. Also, keep samples of students' work (with the date on it). This helps when you are looking at the progress the student has made. The parents might have some questions about the work the student is doing, and it is easier to have a discussion when you have actual material to show. Also, in the file, keep a record of the student's token economy progress (see page 35). You should also keep the record on a spreadsheet each week. If you need to refer to it, it is much easier when you don't have to hunt for the information. This spreadsheet shows that the student has or hasn't followed directions and what kind of "fines" the student has had to pay. All of this is useful to have in a face-to-face conference with the parents or even on a phone conference.

Talking with Parents at a Conference

When discussing a student's issue during a conference, you don't always have to agree with the parent and the parent doesn't always have to agree with you. This does not mean any team member is less important, and just because you disagree with the parent doesn't mean that you shouldn't respect their point of view. Listen to them attentively and make sure they feel heard by saying things such as: "I hear what you are saying." "I understand that you are upset." "Thank you for sharing your input. I will consider that for the future." Sometimes a parent may just need to vent and they want you to listen. They might not want you to take any action other than to hear what they are saying.

Setting Limits

If you feel that there may be some conflict during a conference, always ask an administrator to be there. It is easier to set up the support before the conflict occurs than after it happens. Also, if it gets too heated or takes too long, don't feel bad about stopping the meeting and setting up another time to reconvene. I didn't know if this was acceptable when I first started, and after a couple of three-hour parent conferences, I realized that we were not making any progress and we all were pretty tired and frustrated when we left. This is not an effective way to hold a meeting, so I announced at the beginning of the meeting that if it went over ninety minutes, we would need to reconvene in order to come to decisions in the best interest of the student. I think everyone was relieved when I said this.

It's Okay to Not Know Everything

Also, don't commit to anything if you don't have all the information you need, and never feel bad about telling the parent that you need to investigate it more. It is better to make an informed decision than an incompetent one. If possible, find out if the parent has concerns before the meeting through a phone call. You can tell them that you want to be prepared and bring the information that they might need to the meeting rather than having to call for another meeting after you gather this information. Everyone can appreciate this because no one wants to go to more meetings than necessary.

Support: A Two-Way Street

By establishing a rapport with parents, you are actually including them in your own support system. If you need materials for the class, you could ask parents for suggestions on how to get them. Some of the parents came up with great ideas! When you are feeling discouraged or frustrated about your teaching, you could call up some parents to brag about their child. After an uplifting conversation with them, you will usually feel a lot better about what you are doing. If a student is struggling in your class, sometimes the parents could give some insight into why this behavior is occurring, which could help you find a solution to the problem. By doing this, you won't feel like you are alone and trying to solve all the problems by yourself.

Knowing that you are not alone in being responsible for the success of your student will help you feel less overwhelmed. I remember feeling, as a new teacher, that I wanted to solve all of my students' problems and make them all successful! I knew this was an unrealistic goal, but I couldn't help feeling this way. This is a natural feeling for most new teachers. When we graduate from college, we have this false sense of power and ability. We think we know something that none of the previous teachers know and we are going to make the biggest difference in this student's life. The confidence is a wonderful feeling, and it is good for teachers to feel this way as long as they eventually come back to reality and know that this is an impossible goal for them to reach.

It is important to know that it will take a team to help students be successful and not just the actions of one person. Knowing that you are a part of your student's success will help you focus on your strengths and what you need to do from your perspective. It is helpful to know that you can use parents as a resource when you need to. You can bounce ideas off of them and discuss possibilities because you all have the same goal in mind. You might suggest something that they have already tried and they could tell you if it had worked or not. If it hadn't worked, then you don't need to waste your time trying it and can move on to something else that might work. Or parents might like a strategy that you suggest and will help you fine-tune it because they know their child better than you do.

Once parents realize that you are not in adversarial roles and are instead supportive roles for each other, you can do amazing things together. Sometimes you may have a parent call you who needs your support because they were frustrated. It is during these phone calls that you can remind the parent of the positive things you've seen the student do and how much progress the student has made. Remind them that success is not something that happens overnight and could be a lifelong process. Everyone just needs to celebrate the positive movements that occur.

Diffusing Conflicts

One year a parent had an issue with something that happened in my class that day. I had a nail technician come in and talk about nail hygiene. After her talk, she gave all of the students a manicure and put nail polish on the girls' nails. A student with Down syndrome wanted nail polish on his nails and got very upset when I wouldn't let him have any. Even the other students tried to discourage him but he still got upset, so I allowed the nail technician to put white nail polish on his nails and he was happy. He was such a sweet boy and I didn't like seeing him upset. When he got home, his mother felt that by allowing him to get the nail polish on his nails I was giving other students another reason to make fun of him. She felt comfortable enough to call me and let me know that she was angry. I let her explain why she was angry and then I explained what happened in class. By the end of our conversation, we realized that the situation was just the cause of a misunderstanding and we both worked to clear it up so it wouldn't occur in the future. Since the parent was able to work it out with me, she didn't feel a need to go to an administrator and I was glad that the situation wasn't blown out of proportion. I believe that if she had not been able to talk to me, this could have ended up in a bad situation with a lot of bad feelings. Instead, it turned out well and, years later, I'm still in touch with this family.

If the parents call to set up a meeting, it is all right to ask them if there is a specific issue that they would like to address. Explain that this will help you be better prepared for the meeting and you can invite other people who may be helpful or bring any documentation that will help resolve the issue. If they don't want to tell you the issue, that is also okay.

When you meet parents who are angry, remember to take a deep breath and remind yourself that the parents are angry because they love their child. They not only want to protect and help their child but they want you to feel the same way they do. If you know ahead of time that you are going to meet with parents who are angry, you should ask an administrator or guidance counselor to be with you when you meet with them. If you are alone with the parents and you feel threatened or uncomfortable at any time during the meeting, it is okay to stop the meeting and explain that you need to ask an administrator to join. Step away from the table, calm down, and find an administrator. Explain the situation and ask the administrator to help mediate.

If parents are angry, the first thing you should do is allow them to share why they feel this way without interrupting them, even if you disagree with them and some of the things they say. You can take notes of things you want to address when it is your turn to speak. When they are done, let them know you hear what they are saying and understand how they are feeling. Restating their problem in your own words is a way to show them that you were listening to them. If you don't know about the incident they are talking about, agree that you will investigate it and get back to them. Make sure that you do get back to them in a timely manner and document that you did. Ask the parents what they want you to do to resolve the problem. If their suggestion is feasible and agreeable to all, then follow through with it and then let them know the problem has been resolved. If their suggestion is not feasible, explain why. Sometimes they don't know how to resolve the problem and you can work as a team to come up with solutions. Make sure you speak calmly and don't take anything personally even if it feels like they are putting you on the defensive. Try to imagine how you would act if you were in their shoes and this was your child.

Handling Threats

If you are threatened by a parent, immediately involve your administrator. One year I had a mother threaten me by saying that if I didn't give her son a better grade, her husband who was a state highway trooper would give me a ticket whenever he saw me on the road. At first I was scared and then I was angry. Instead of giving in to her demands, my administrator called both parents in for a meeting. The husband was extremely upset that his wife threatened me and said that he would have to report it to his supervisor and would be transferred out of the area. I accepted his apology, but I did not change his child's grade. Sometimes the only way to face something like this is head-on and always involving your administration.

Don't Overshare

Be careful about discussing another teacher's actions with the parents. You don't want to throw another colleague under the bus and you wouldn't want someone to do that to you. It is better to be prepared in case you are faced with this situation. If a parent says they are having a problem with another teacher, suggest that the parent call the school counselor to discuss possible solutions. Explain that you are not in a position to discuss another teacher. You can discuss things that the student could do in order to be more successful in another class, but don't guarantee that these things will work.

Also, be very careful about discussing another student with someone else's parents. Confidentiality rules can be very tricky and strict. You should never mention another student's name in your conversation with parents. Make it a practice to say "another student" and if asked for a name, explain that they wouldn't like you to use their child's name with another parent, so you try to respect this with all conversations. You don't want to start with one problem and then end up with more because you mentioned other names. If parents hear you mention other students' names, they may wonder if you are mentioning their child's name to others. Parents respect you more when they know that you will stick to your principle of confidentiality. They know then that you will respect their child's identity as well.

Don't Undershare Either

Once, a parent was praising me for staying in close contact with her, and attributed her child's success to our communication. She was disturbed that her child's other teachers did not do the same. Even though I know this made the other teachers uncomfortable, I was not going to apologize for my own success. This system worked for me, but may not for other teachers. I can't speak for them and can only control my own actions.

Reluctant Parents

There are many reasons parents are reluctant to be more involved and it is important to understand why. Many teachers assume parents don't care, but over the years, in all the years I've taught, I've never met a parent that didn't care about their children. Many parents hold more than one job and are exhausted just keeping food on the table. Others have so many children that it is hard to have the energy to motivate all of them to excel in school. Some parents are extremely frustrated and don't know what else to do. It is imperative for you to determine a communication process that works for them. Ask if you can leave a voicemail or email them weekly to let them know how their child is doing. Let them know that it is okay if they don't respond immediately but it would help you to know that they got your message. Explain that if you do have a problem, you will need to discuss it with them but that you also like to brag about their child. After a few positive phone calls, the parents won't be so reluctant to talk to you.

Helicopter Parents

You will get some of those parents that tend to hover over their children. Remember they do this because they love their child. It's possible that they may not have had good experiences with the education system in the past. Reassure these parents that you will be in regular contact. Even set up a weekly schedule to contact them and make sure that you do this so they can learn to trust you. Give them a contact number and email address where they can reach you. Eventually you can ease up on contacting them and only call them every two weeks and eventually once a month. They will ease up when they learn they can trust you to be available when necessary.

Listen to their suggestions because they know their child better than you do and their input may actually help you in the classroom. Offer suggestions for them to use at home to help their child with their academic work. If you disagree with what they are saying but it requires no action on your part, just let them know that you hear them and you appreciate their input. If they want you to do something that you don't agree with, tell them that you appreciate their input and you will discuss it with your administrator. If they continue to insist that you do something you don't agree with and you have already discussed this with your administrator, it is time to set up a conference with the parents and administrator.

In this chapter, you learned about:
- Working with parents to make a team effort
- Getting accurate contact info and making contact with parents
- Giving positive reports—not just bad ones
- Handling the not-so-good reports
- Getting ahead of problems
- Planning and attending conferences with parents
- Managing support: a two-way street
- Diffusing conflicts with parents
- Oversharing and undersharing
- Getting reluctant or busy parents involved
- Handling helicopter parents

Conclusion

Teaching is the most wonderful profession in the world! I have never regretted a minute of time I spent learning how to teach and then teaching students for more than thirty years. If you want to make a difference, this is the profession for you.

That said, teaching is not for the faint-hearted. There may be times when you are tired and frustrated and everything is not rosy and perfect, but you need to remember that you are touching lives and impacting futures. One year at graduation, one of my students handed me a box of long-stemmed roses as a thank-you and I was moved to tears. When I thanked his family for the flowers too, his mom let me know that it was all his idea because I had helped him and never gave up on him when others had.

It is so rewarding when former students see me out in public and reintroduce themselves. Most of the time I remember them, but after so many years, I recognize their faces even if I can't remember their names. I love the stories they tell me about what they are doing at the present, and they love to recall memories of their time in my class. It is so heartwarming when I realize that what I did made an impact on their lives even if I didn't know it at the time.

Being an effective teacher takes hard work. It won't happen overnight. It takes years of practice and adjusting how you teach. If something isn't working after you have tried it for a while, there is no shame in scrapping that strategy and looking for something else.

But you won't be alone. Helping a student succeed in your classroom is not an individual activity. It is more like a team sport and you are one of the team players. Your team should consist of the student, the parent, you, the student's other teachers, and the administration, as well as any other personnel that work with the student. Everyone plays an important role in helping the student succeed in your class and in the future.

Professional development should be a constant practice. You should always want to improve and be a better teacher. Never stop learning. Always strive to find a new way that you may be able to reach your students. Remember that you can always learn a new strategy or technique that might help your students. You can learn from experienced teachers and new teachers too. Be open to new ideas.

When you start feeling like you are heading down a trend of negative thinking, you need to make a mental effort to regroup. Find positive people to be around. Find an outside activity to relieve stress. Find ways to reenergize without beating yourself up for being discouraged. This is a normal feeling, but don't allow yourself to wallow too long in your pity party. Accept it and then work to move in a positive direction.

All of the things I talk about in this book are going to take conscious effort until they become second nature. Rest assured though, one day you will be doing many of the things I mention—as well as your own tricks and strategies—without even having to think about them. Sometimes you might return to chapters to refresh your memory or even get new ideas.

Even though I gave some sample activities that seem geared to a specific age group, they can all be adjusted depending on the age level you teach. There are so many great ideas online and among your colleagues. Take the time to exchange them. When you respect your colleagues and students and gain their respect, learning new things together can be a lot of fun.

Remember to be fair and consistent with your discipline. Students don't need you to be their friend. They have enough friends. They need someone to lead them in the right direction. Also, remember that you can't save everyone, but you have to give it your best shot. You will affect students' lives, even though you may never see the outcomes.

Build your own support system. You don't want to feel isolated with the weight of the world on your shoulders. Talking things over with others really helps. Just remember that your support system may change over time. My support system consisted of my family, friends who were not educators, colleagues in the education field, and parents of students.

There may come a time when you need to think about transferring to a new school for the next year. Your present school may not be the right fit for you. It is okay to feel this way. You may end up staying too long in one place and feel that you are getting stale and need a new environment to recharge your teaching. Starting at a new school can be scary and exciting at the same time. It also keeps you on your toes with learning new procedures and new colleagues. Every time I have moved to a new school, I felt like I had a fresh new start. I used each move to learn new things from new colleagues. Having taught in five different schools in my career, I can look back and say that even though the moves were stressful, each one helped me become a stronger and more effective teacher.

Even though there are so many things involved in the art of teaching, don't forget that teaching should be fun. Not only should it be fun for the students but fun for you. Teaching, like any other profession, is what you make of it. If you just go through the motions and do it just to get a paycheck, the shine will wear off quickly. If you put a lot into it, you will get a lot out of it.

When you discover the joy of teaching, teaching will be a joy!

Appendix I:
Scrapbooking Instructions

1. Double click on Adobe Photoshop
2. Click on "File"
3. Click on "New"
4. Type in the name of your file
5. Make sure width is 8.5 inches and height is 11 inches
6. Click on "Transparent"
7. Click "OK"
8. Click on header bar to move page over
9. Click on "Layer"
10. Click on "New"
11. Click on "Layer"
12. Type in "Background"
13. Click on "OK"
14. Click on "Foreground Color" on tool bar
15. Pick a color and click "OK"
16. Click on "Paintbucket" on tool bar
17. Click on your page
18. Click "Filter"
19. Click "Texture"
20. Click "Texturizer"
21. Pick a texture and click "OK"
22. Click "File"
23. Click "Open"
24. Find your picture and click on it to open it
25. Click on header bar to move picture over
26. Click on "Move" tool (arrow with cross) on tool bar
27. Left click on picture and hold down as you move it to your page
28. Maximize your page by clicking the big box on the right corner
29. Hold down "shift" and left click until you see 2 arrows
30. Keep holding down "shift" as you move the corner to change the size

31. Hit enter.
32. Click on picture to move it where you want it
33. Click on "Foreground Color" for color of text
34. Pick a color and click "OK"
35. Click on "T" on the tool bar
36. Click on your page where you want the title
37. Pick font and size
38. Give your page a title
39. Move text to where you want it
40. Click on "Layer"
41. Click on "New"
42. Click on "Layer"
43. Type in "Journaling"
44. Click on "OK"
45. Click on rectangular marquee on the tool bar
46. Left click on your page
47. Hold down left click and move mouse to draw box
48. Click on foreground color on tool bar
49. Pick a color and click "OK"
50. Click on Paintbucket on the tool bar
51. Click on the journaling box
52. Click "Filter"
53. Click "Texture"
54. Click "Texturizer"
55. Pick a texture and click "OK"
56. Click on foreground color for color of text
57. Pick a color and click "OK"
58. Click on "T" on the tool bar
59. Click on your page where you want the information
60. Pick font and size
61. Type the content of your page
62. Move text to where you want it
63. On layer palette, click on layer that is NOT text
64. Click on the "F" at the bottom of the layer palette
65. Click on "drop shadow"
66. Click on "OK"
67. Do this for each layer that is NOT text
68. Save your page in your folder

Appendix II:
Duties of a Paraprofessional

Duties of a Paraprofessional

1. Take attendance on computer and grade book during the first ten minutes of class.
2. Walk around the classroom and make sure students are on task.
3. Answer students' questions.
4. Make copies.
5. File student work and papers.
6. Escort designated students to classes.
7. Attend elective classes with designated students.
8. Escort students who have a detention to the lunchroom and back to class.
9. Work with small groups of students if needed.
10. Enforce classroom rules.
11. Collect homework and documents.
12. Review notes with students if needed.
13. Monitor students if I am called out of the room.
14. Do not use sarcasm or intentionally hurt students' self-esteem.
15. Do not stay with a student in the room by yourself with the classroom doors closed.
16. Stand out in the hallway by classroom door to monitor hallway during class changes.
17. Any additional duties needed by the classroom teacher.

_____

Date

_____

Paraprofessional Signature

_____

Teacher Signature

Appendix III:
The UDL Template

Title of Lesson:

Goals and Objectives:

Student's Name:	*Learning Style	*Learning Style	*Learning Style	Assessment:	Activity 1	Activity 2	Activity 3
Cinderella	V A T K	V A T K	V A T K				
Peter Pan	V A T K	V A T K	V A T K				
Snow White	V A T K	V A T K	V A T K				
Jiminy Cricket	V A T K	V A T K	V A T K				

*Learning Styles Key: V (visual), A (auditory), T (tactile), K (kinesthetic)

INDEX

About the Author

Pat Hensley, MSEd., is a lifelong special education teacher, professor of education at Furman University, and the editor of the website successful-teaching.net. Pat lives with her husband in Greenville, South Carolina. www.successfulteaching.net

MORE GREAT BOOKS

from Little, Brown Lab

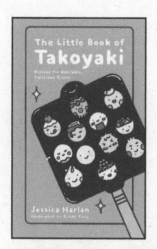

LITTLE, BROWN LAB

www.littlebrownlab.com

facebook • instagram @littlebrownlaboratory